52 Ways to Wow Your Husband

PAM FARREL

HARVEST HOUSE PUBLISHERS

EUGENE, OREGON

Cover design by Left Coast Design, Portland, Oregon

Cover photo © momentimages / Getty Images

Published in association with the literary agency of Alive Communications, Inc., 7680 Goddard Street, Suite 200, Colorado Springs, CO 80920. www.alivecommunications.com.

52 WAYS TO WOW YOUR HUSBAND
Copyright © 2011 by Pam Farrel
Published by Harvest House Publishers
Eugene, Oregon 97402
www.harvesthousepublishers.com

Library of Congress Cataloging-in-Publication Data
Farrel, Pam, 1959-
52 ways to wow your husband / Pam Farrel.
   p. cm.
ISBN 978-0-7369-3780-1 (pbk.)
ISBN 978-0-7369-4194-5 (eBook)
   1. Marriage—Religious aspects—Christianity.   2. Marriage.   3. Husbands—Miscellanea.   4. Husbands—Psychology. I. Title.
BV835.F38 2011
248.8'44—dc22
                                                                                    2011007477

Printed in the United States of America

11 12 13 14 15 16 17 18 19 / BP-NI / 10 9 8 7 6 5 4 3 2 1

To Bill

The man who has wowed me for over thirty-one years.
You always put a smile on my face.
Thank you for loving me. I treasure the privilege of loving you.
Place me like a seal over your heart,
like a seal on your arm;
for love is as strong as death…
It burns like blazing fire,
like a mighty flame.
Many waters cannot quench love;
rivers cannot sweep it away…
Come away, my beloved.

(Song of Solomon 8:6,7,14)

Always, your angel,
Pam

Contents

Introduction

Wow! That is the word my husband, Bill, says anytime something great happens to him, when he loves an activity, and even when he preaches through a passage and something strikes him in a positive way. (Some churches say "Amen" to their pastor; ours learned to reply "Wow!")

When Bill supported me through college, I gave him a tie tack with the word "Wow!" on it. So to wow him has become a synonym for putting a smile on his face. And isn't "Wow!" the response we would like to receive from our man, both inside and outside the bedroom? We love hearing:

"Wow, honey!"

"Wow, that was awesome!"

"Wow, I didn't know life could be so great!"

"Wow, you look hot, babe!"

"Wow, can we do that again?"

"Wow, that was incredible!"

And my favorite, which is as close to speechless as I can write here, "Oh...aaahhhh...wow!" (Panting to catch his breath, followed by a heavy sigh of happy contentment.)

This book is about putting a smile on your husband's face. And the ideas are not just mine. Some are from many of my friends who have vibrant relationships. Some are from those who have worked hard to weather tough marital storms and now have smiles. Still others come from marriage experts who also enjoy wowing their husbands.

The wow principles also come from over thirty years in the trenches helping real couples stay in love for a lifetime. Guys have been telling us for years the things that drain their love tank, things that drive them nuts, and what reignites, reenergizes, and reinvigorates their ability to give and receive love. So this book is a glimpse behind the curtains of a man's heart and life.

The layout is simple—one wow idea a week for an entire year. This could become the best year of your husband's life (and the best year of your life!). Each entry contains a *Wow Idea*, followed by a *Wow Assignment* to help you think how you might make some change or apply the concept in your own life.

Then comes a *Wow Wisdom* section that helps you partner with God to gain the power, motivation, or insight to actually accomplish the wow. I know God wants to help you. He's given us ample evidence that He is the absolute professional when it comes to making love work. The Bible says "God is love" (1 John 4:8), and inscribed on the wedding gifts Bill and I exchanged was "We love because [God] first loved us" (1 John 4:19). So I know you will be in great hands if you simply ask God to "help a girl out." He will spark even more ideas on how to wow your man. (God created your guy so He knows what he likes!)

Finally, I have included a *Wow Date* idea, which is something to get your wheels turning and show you one way you can apply the wow principle for the week that might put a smile on your man's face.

All the wows are not about sex (as you might think), but plenty of red-hot monogamy ideas are included to keep that spark, sizzle, and pizzazz—that wow—in the bedroom. Many of the ideas are wows that go a little deeper into a man's heart and soul so the wow results will linger and that smile will last beyond just the date. We want that smile to stick and the love to stay.

Feel free to adapt, tweak, springboard off these ideas wherever your imagination can take you. This is your book. I suggest you not announce to your man that you are going to wow him once a week, every week. Instead, *just do it*. You want to surprise him with the wows rather than set up expectations. Mark up the book, jot down ideas on sticky notes, log thoughts onto your calendar or into your Outlook.

You don't have to do the wows in the order they appear in the book; feel free to do them in the order you think would best wow your man. He might need to get used to you wanting to wow him. So feel free to begin simply and build to some big wow date for special days like his birthday, Valentine's Day, your anniversary, or a vacation.

Don't get discouraged if he is not as wowed about some of the ideas as he is others. Just seeing what he responds to is its own payoff. After this year, you'll have a great catalog of information on exactly what wows your guy. Be sure to mark down or star in the book those wows that get the best response so you can re-create them or remold them in a slightly varied way in the years to come.

You might want to gather your girlfriends or your sisters and sisters-in-law and make a pact to make this the year to wow your men. Each of you should have your own copy of *52 Ways to Wow Your Husband* and encourage each other to keep up the race to win and wow your man's heart. It isn't a competition, just a group to encourage you to keep up the great work. You might want to meet weekly and pray for each other's marriages and your men—and yourselves. Be sure to maintain your marital privacy and don't give away all the juicy details! The nuances of the wow are a secret between you and your man. However, you are more likely to complete all 52 wows if you have at least one friend or mentor holding you accountable and cheering you on.

I want to encourage you too. Keep checking our website at www.Love-Wise.com. We have articles and other books with more romantic ideas (*Red-Hot Monogamy* has over 200 red-hot ideas). We also have ongoing e-news that will contain even more ways to wow your guy, so be sure to sign up at www.Love-wise.com to stay connected or to come do a wow date or event with us! Success is easier if you are surrounded by those who also want to have a love that wows for a lifetime.

Mostly, have fun. It's a thrill to wow your guy and a joy to see that smile on his face!

The Recharger Box

What a man finds romantic is a woman who will lower his stress! In *Men Are Like Waffles—Women Are Like Spaghetti*, I explain that men go to their favorite easy boxes to rest and recharge. God helped us women recognize these easy boxes in that most of them are shaped like boxes—the TV screen, the newspaper, the garage, the Xbox, the computer screen, the football field, the baseball diamond, the basketball court, the refrigerator, and the bed. The bed box (also known as the sex box) is a husband's favorite box to go to when he is stressed out. This box or square is kind of like the center square on a bingo card, and a man can get to that box from every other square on his waffle.

Wow Assignment

Find out your man's favorite easy box he goes to for recharging. Here are some ways to discover this vital information:

- If given thirty minutes of dead time, what does he do?
- If he were given a day off, where would he like to go?
- What does he do now when stressed?
- What does he watch on TV when relaxing? (Sports? Movies? Adventures? Fix-it shows?)

Kendra Smiley and her husband, John, wrote *Do Your Kids a Favor…
Love Your Spouse*. John was wowed unexpectedly by Kendra with his all-
time favorite box:

> I've been a Green Bay Packers fan for years and transferred
> that enthusiasm to our three teenage sons. I never imag-
> ined I would actually be able to see a game at Lambeau
> Field because legend has it that the only way to get tickets
> is to inherit them when someone dies. But legends don't
> stop Kendra! She called the ticket office, asking about the
> purchase of five tickets for the last home game of the sea-
> son. After the laughter died down (I guess there was some
> truth to the legend), they referred her to an agency offering
> "Weekend Packages." She knew we couldn't afford all the
> extras of a package, and somehow she managed to convince
> the woman at that office to simply sell her five tickets. She
> gave me a gift that took her time, her effort, and a little bit of
> her charming persuasion. What a great model for our kids!

My man's favorite easy box is: _____.

Wow Wisdom

Pray and thank God for your husband. Often we women push,
push, push our spouse to be more productive or work on our "honey-
do" list even on his day off. If you keep pushing, he might begin to see
you as a mother or a boss, not a wife and lover. A husband who gets
pushed to do too many things he doesn't enjoy will exhaust himself
emotionally and grow distant from his wife. Think about how much
better your life is when you are connected with your lover!

Instead of resenting your "waffleman" for needing to recharge, thank
God he has a box to recharge in so he can maintain the energy to keep
up with you! As Paul reminds us, "In everything give thanks" (1 Thes-
salonians 5:18 NASB).

Wow Date

Make him breakfast in bed and serve waffles. Give him a note for one free day off to do whatever he wants—to enjoy his favorite "waffle box(es)." Include a gift card for something that helps him recharge. While you're there in bed, why not enjoy some "bingo"? Remember, for most men, bingo is the number one recharger box.

Wow 2

Say Yes

Ginger Kolbaba, editor of the online magazine *Kyria*, offers the following great insight:

> "No, no way," my mind screamed. But then I did something insane. I looked into my husband's eyes. So he didn't think through all the logistics; he had tried to do something good, something fun for us as a couple. And I had the power to cut him down, crush his excitement, to penalize him for the adventure he'd tried to bring to our relationship. And that's when I learned an important marriage lesson. Sometimes it is better to say yes, even when you want to, even when you are justified to say no. Frankly, it is about the good of the marriage, not only about the individuals who make up that marriage...My first instinct was to say no...But the grace of God got through my thick skull and reminded me of the importance of saying yes.[1]

Wow Assignment

This week, try to say yes as much as you possibly can to your husband. If what he asks you to do is *not* immoral, illegal, or life-threatening, say yes. Give it a wholehearted, enthusiastic yes!

Wow Wisdom

Here's the trick. You might have been saying no for so long, your husband is afraid to ask anything of you anymore. He might be so withdrawn from your predictable no answers that he doesn't even make a request or an invitation. If this is the case, you might offer a yes. For example, "Honey, you know how you asked me over and over to go deep-sea fishing with you? Well, I want you know that if you asked again, I'd say yes. In fact, I have the boat captain's number right here, and I have this Saturday free if you want to go right away. No pressure, I just wanted you to know." Then give a kiss, slide the number into his front pants pocket, and leave the room. If you flirt a little, your yes will seem more believable.

Wow Date

Jump-start the new "yes atmosphere" of your marriage by planning a date full of yeses. Do a few things your husband loves that you have said no to in the past. Go running *with* him, go to the gym *with* him, go to the hardware store *with* him. Say yes to that fast car or ski boat (rent one just for a day!). Be his friend, his buddy, his pal, his lover, and revel in saying yes to his ideas all through the date.

Wow 3

New Attitude

Mom was worried that her twin boys, age six, had developed extreme personalities—one was a total pessimist, the other a total optimist. So she took them to a psychiatrist.

First the psychiatrist treated the pessimist. Trying to brighten his outlook, the psychiatrist took him to a room piled to the ceiling with brand-new toys. But instead of yelping with delight, the little boy burst into tears.

"What's the matter?" the psychiatrist asked, baffled. "Don't you want to play with any of the toys?"

"Yes," the little boy bawled, "but if I did, I'd only break them."

Next the psychiatrist treated the optimist. Trying to dampen his outlook, the psychiatrist took him to a room piled to the ceiling with horse manure. But instead of wrinkling his nose in disgust, the optimist emitted a yelp of delight. He dropped to his knees and began gleefully digging out scoop after scoop with his bare hands.

"What do you think you're doing?" the psychiatrist asked.

"With all this manure," the little boy replied, beaming, "there must be a pony in here somewhere."[2]

Wow Assignment

Are you feeling blue? Acknowledge that depression can weigh heavy on a marriage. One husband cornered me in the lobby after church and said, "I don't know what to do. My wife is just so sad all the time. I've tried everything! I am so exhausted. I'm holding her up, the housework, my job, the kids. I can't keep going this way."

The first step in wowing your man might be to own that you are depressed and need to take action to improve your own mental and emotional wellness.

Wow Wisdom

My friend K!mberly is a missionary in Singapore. She and her husband, James, have faithfully served the people of the Pacific Rim for over twenty years. K!mberly is fluent in Mandarin. They have lived and worked overseas, far from their very American upbringing, for most of her adult life.

But K!mberly, as any woman might, missed home. In 2001 she hit a wall of depression so strong she sought medical help. During this time, with a diagnosis of a chronic low serotonin level, she decided for the sake of herself, her marriage, and her family that she needed to reclaim her happiness.

K!mberly had heard my message "Choosin' Joy" during the year she was turning forty. She chose to replace the *i* in her name with an exclamation mark, so each time she wrote her name she would remember God is the *!* (the excitement in life). She wanted a daily reminder that there is much more to look forward to. James has benefited greatly from the *!*.

Be proactive with your emotional health. See a doctor, exercise, pray this verse as a reminder that God is your *!*:

> But You, LORD, are a shield around me,
>> my glory, the One who lifts my head high.
>>> (Psalm 3:3)

Wow Date

Create a marker, like the exclamation point in K!mberly's name. Choose something that will remind you that God can and will be the One who can give back your hope and joy. Make it personal, such as a letter in your name or a new signature. Or get a ring or bracelet you see consistently. It can also be a screen saver, a ringtone, or a poster—something you see or hear daily.

Plan a cozy date in a quiet place and share the marker with your husband. Take him off the hook. God sent him to be your partner, not your therapist and not the one responsible for making you happy. Only you and God can accomplish that. Use this date to thank your man for caring, but free him from the pressure of having to make you happy.

Wow 4

Wedding Gifts

I asked a simple question of my Facebook friends: "What was the best wedding gift you were given that now, years later, has an impact?"

Kathy: My kitchen wouldn't be the same without my Cutco knives (bought with money from my maternal Gmom), my now-cracked pottery duck utensil holder, and my ceramic mixing bowls (from Tom's grandmother). These gifts were given to us at our wedding shower for the "wedding dress rehearsal" six years before the actual date. By the time we actually got married, my grandmother had passed. It still is special to have that gift from her.

Lynette: The honor of your husband as our officiate/pastor marrying us.

Lanette: A Bible with our names on it!

Kelli: (1) The wedding dress that my sister handmade for me and paid for out of her own pocket; (2) the video that my aunt and uncle recorded of my entire wedding.

Cheri: Family Bible.

Dawn: Pre-wedding gift: My parents lived on the other side of the United States (Florida), and their involvement in the wedding included a long, expensive drive to California where my husband-to-be lived. My mother-in-love stepped into my mom's place to help me pick out my dress, cake, flowers, photos, church/reception—everything! I would have been lost without her loving help. Such a gracious woman.

These are all wonderful and sentimental, but my favorite is:

Dan: My wife, Joanne!

Wow Assignment

Think back to when you were newlyweds. What were your favorite gifts then and what has lasted in its meaning? Take that walk down memory lane again. This time, pull out your wedding album and the photos of your early years together. How was life different then from how it is now? Are there any changes you want to make that would make it feel as if you were newlyweds again? Or if you are a newlywed, as you look at those who have been married longer than you, what do you observe? Which couples have marriages you want to emulate?

Wow Wisdom

Pray that God gives you that same longing to be together as you had as a newlywed.

> The man said,
> "This is now bone of my bones
> and flesh of my flesh;
> she shall be called 'woman,'
> for she was taken out of man."
> That is why a man leaves his father and mother and is
> united to his wife, and they become one flesh.
> (Genesis 2:23-24)

Wow Date

Take a moment and write down what a typical day looked like in your first year of marriage. Ours was something like this:

- Cuddle in bed *together* as long as possible.
- Shower *together*.
- Drive to work *together*.
- Zip home to be *together* at lunch for a quickie. (Who needs food?)
- Work but think about how you can't wait to be *together*.
- Make dinner *together*.
- Do something fun like work out *together*, shop *together*, or do ministry *together*.
- Come home and jump into bed for some red-hot monogamy *together*!

Set aside a day this week to be newlyweds again. Plan a date to be *together*! Do some things you loved as newlyweds and do them again—*together*!

Wow 5

Grab a Cup of Identity

My husband, Bill, loves his coffee. But along with Bill's love of coffee, he also has a habit that could be very annoying. He seems to have an aversion to putting the coffee mugs into the dishwasher. I find coffee cups every place imaginable: in the garage, in the car, in the truck, in the closet, on the sidewalk, on the deck and patio, in the shop, in the office, on the stairwell, in the bathroom. You name the place, and I have likely found a coffee cup there. It's a good thing we are authors and speakers because we love collecting coffee mugs from all the churches we speak at and all the TV and radio shows we appear on—and we need every one of them!

Wow Assignment

I'm not a coffee drinker really. I might drink a nonfat latte now and then, but coffee makes my heart race, and I prefer that only Bill makes my heart skip a beat! Bill says that I am naturally caffeinated by God, and it takes Bill three cups of coffee just to keep up with my energy. Bill has an internal homing device that helps him spot a Starbucks green awning. Coffee is a part of what makes Bill…well, Bill! What's one quirky trait of your husband's identity?

Wow Wisdom

One day when we were moving out of one home into another, I was doing a last load of dishes, and I realized it was composed of all coffee mugs. Forty-seven of them, to be exact. It made me smile because years ago, I decided to pray for Bill every time I saw one of his empty displaced mugs. I was seeking to apply the principle "love each other deeply, because love covers over a multitude of sins" (1 Peter 4:8). I have embraced the ever-reappearing dirty coffee mug with fond affection because it reminds me of my hard workin' man who requires caffeine to do all the wonderful acts of service that benefit so many, including me.

Wow Date

For Bill's fiftieth birthday, we celebrated by having him select and roast his own brand of coffee. It took one afternoon to visit a coffee farm, select the beans, roast them to perfection, then design the label. I knew I had a winning date as he sat, lingered a moment to savor the aroma of his Farrel Family blend of Mountain Thunder Vienna roast. He took a sip, and I watched a big grin appear on my husband's well-caffeinated soul.

Think of a way to plan a date that celebrates something that is a representation of your man.

Wow 6

Small Things

At a marriage conference, the question was asked, "What makes you feel intimate with your spouse? What gift does he or she give that makes you feel loved?"

The couples faced each other, held hands, and shared heart-to-heart, soul-to-soul. Bill also opened up to me, and among the long list he reeled off was a very simple but important item: "When you get my coffee right. Black with real cream, no sugar, no whip, no flavored creamer substitutes."

Got it, Babe! Love to you is a mug of the house blend with the real moo juice cream in a cup, not a travel mug, because you love the way it smells and the feel of the steam as you sip it from a real coffee cup.

Love is in the details, in the small things—the nuances of affection. Love is translated, "You noticed the subtleties, and you cared enough to act."

Wow Assignment

Begin taking notes of the small things about your man and his likes. What is his favorite:

Food?
Aroma?
Office pen?
Aftershave or cologne?
Tool or gadget?
Clothing company?
Athletic gear brand?
Beverage?
Restaurant?

Wow Wisdom

God asks, "Who dares despise the day of small things?" (Zechariah 4:10). We can ask ourselves a similar question: *Am I despising the small things that matter to my mate?* I believe God wants me to care about the small things in Bill's world, and you to care about the small things in your man's world, because those small things matter to him.

Wow Date

Today turn the small things into a big wow for your man! Review your notes about his loves and likes, and create a date of favorites. String together small acts of service and care all day. Do the small gestures of affection: bring in the paper for him, make his coffee or favorite breakfast, send his favorite snack to his office or meet him at his favorite restaurant for lunch, bake his favorite cookie or dessert, make that favorite meal or midnight snack. Talk about his favorite topics, sit with him and watch a favorite TV program, or arrange to do one of his favorite activities. And consider topping off the evening by giving him sex his favorite way.

Then try something radical. Keep observing those little things and keep looking for new ways to acknowledge, enjoy, and fulfill them. Let the small nuances of devotion add up in a big way to stoke the fires of your love.

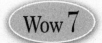

Hold Me Up, Honey

Janet Holm McHenry, author of *PrayerWalk: Becoming a Woman of Prayer, Strength, and Discipline,* shares the key to wowing your man in the midst of the unwelcome, unwanted, and unreal circumstances you might find yourself and your marriage in:

> One way I try to hold my husband up is to walk and pray for him—prayerwalk. As I'm walking I think about his needs and the demands on him as a cattle rancher. While we don't live on the ranch, I do occasionally walk the ranch…God gives me insight into my husband, and I pray accordingly.
>
> "Lord," I'll pray, "give him strength and favor. Help his equipment to work today without any breakdowns." I also pray that his cattle stay healthy—that there not be any deaths, especially during the challenging winters we face in our valley that is at five thousand feet in the California Sierra Nevada.

One winter God didn't answer the part of the prayer about the cows. Janet continues:

> Five calves and an old bull bedded down during a blizzard

in a dry creek bed, got covered over with snow, and died. They were at a remote corner of the ranch, so Craig didn't know they were there, but a disgruntled neighbor called animal control and soon Craig was charged with seven felonies related to animal abuse. The district attorney alleged that Craig had not fed his cattle, even though a necropsy (autopsy on an animal) proved that one calf had twenty pounds of feed in its stomach and the other animal tested had a high level of colostrum (mother's milk).

The case was delayed for three and a half years. Stress by then was really high; the legal expenses were in the tens of thousands and we had just gotten two kids through college and our third was in his freshman year. By then I was prayerwalking not only for justice for my husband but for my marriage—I was hurting so much that my respect and love for him were fading.

Wow Assignment

What is weighing heavy on your man's heart? Begin making his worry your prayer.

Wow Wisdom

Janet looked for more help for her prayers:

> I kind of fell apart for the two months between the trial and the sentencing. It was hard to pray, so I turned to a dear devotional book, *Streams in the Desert* by L.B. Cowman, and allowed the author's choice of scripture and her own words to become my prayers. I read portions of the book to Craig as we drove to the sentencing in July 2005. With each scripture that I turned into prayer, Craig breathed a huge breath, as though he were giving control to God.

Tune in to the next *Wow* to see how the story ends.

Wow Date

Take your husband on a prayer walk. Pick him up from work, pack a picnic, and head to one of his favorite outdoor spots. Pray as you walk, or pray as you sit—but pray for what is on his heart. If you want to add to the comfort, give him a foot rub, temple massage, or sit in the Jacuzzi and simply listen to him spill his woes.

Wow 8

Keep Praying

It is often darkest right before the dawn, as Janet learned:

> During the two-week trial, it was clear the judge had already determined my husband's guilt. He badgered my husband's witnesses on the stand, would not allow some of the evidence to be introduced, and also refused to allow Craig's best witness to testify. Consequently, Craig was convicted on six of the felonies. I was devastated.

Wow Assignment

If you and your husband find yourselves in difficult circumstances, pray and ask God for His view of what you are facing. Pray not for the circumstance (of course you and your man want it to change), but pray for your ability to handle it, and pray for your mate's stamina to deal with it. Janet continues:

> At the sentencing, friends of ours, including several pastors, filled the courtroom. The judge pronounced his sentence— four years of probation and a fine in the tens of thousands of dollars. Craig could not leave the state. He could not

own a firearm. He could not practice law (he is also an attorney himself), nor teach (he was working on a doctorate so he could teach political science at the college level). After the hearing, Craig was surrounded by our friends who said: "Craig was such an example of how a Christian should behave under such circumstances." "Craig was amazing in court!" "Aren't you proud of your husband?"

He had been amazing throughout the trial—an example of utter trust in God, even through the end. I realized then that God *had* answered my prayer—he had renewed my love and respect for my husband.

Wow Wisdom

Janet shares the powerful result of praying from God's point of view:

> Over the next two years Craig and I worked as a team preparing his appeal. About a year and a half after the sentencing, Craig's conviction was overturned by the California Court of Appeals. As I look back on that rough time in our marriage, I know now that God allowed it to help develop a love and respect for my husband that was rock solid.

Wow Date

Make a prayer date. If your husband is comfortable with prayer, take several verses and walk and pray those verses over him. If he is new to prayer or uncomfortable, simply walk hand-in-hand and ask, "Honey, I know things are heavy on your heart, and I want to help. How can I pray for you today?" If your husband is ambivalent, pray silently as you walk and simply give him a hug. Say something like, "I love you. I am praying things get better because I really love and care for you."

Consider a prayer gift, perhaps one of the verses you will continue to pray on a framed plaque, a bookmark, or a coffee mug. Consider adding to the prayer by going to a favorite spot that helps him feel close to God or more at peace, wherever that may be—fishing a stream, sailing the ocean, standing on a mountaintop, riding the range, or sitting in a chapel. A simple gesture of love is to scratch his back as you whisper prayers of blessing over his life.

Wow 9

Intimacy 101

Catherine and Rick Weber teach couples enrichment classes on "The Secrets to Love, Sex, and Happiness." They have been happily married for twenty-five years, and they help others stay happily married for decades, so they are experts on wowing each other. Dr. Weber is a PhD and an accomplished researcher and author, and she has empirical evidence on what really wows the brain:

> What wows a man anyway? What memories make a lasting impression and impact on your man's brain and heart? Mostly, it's Love. Pleasure. Happiness. What hits the spot is different for everyone, so we need to ask to find out what it is for our husbands...
>
> When we have positive, emotionally enjoyable experiences, they wow us, and we remember them. Research shows that what is most memorable in the brain, and what makes us most happy, are experiences that create meaningful memories that can live on in our mind...Memorable times together make a lasting impact on our minds and hearts.[3]

Wow Assignment

Catherine continues,

> There are a few times that stand out for Rick. A few years
> ago, I was willing to spontaneously go to San Francisco to
> celebrate our anniversary—without the children. We went
> on spontaneous adventures, discovering and enjoying the
> days as they unfolded. Then, for his fortieth birthday, I
> helped him plan a golfing day with some guy friends, and a
> few more friends joining us for an electric boat ride around
> the New Port Beach harbor for a sunset picnic dinner.
>
> These were special occasions when I went out of my way
> to do something that we wouldn't usually do, that would
> be enjoyable for him.

Recently Catherine asked Rick, "What can I do to wow you more?"
His eyes lit up. "Anything? In my wildest dreams? You could surprise
me with tickets to the Lakers and Boston Celtics playoff game. Attend
other sporting events with me (and be somewhat enthusiastic about
it). You could learn to play golf and tennis with me."

Notice the element of surprise?

Danielle Turner, a member of the department of psychiatry at
Cambridge University, contends that the element of surprise helps
you become memorable: "Researchers at Cambridge University coined
a term 'super-learning.' They showed that if you are 'super-surprised'
you will super-learn. That is, the more unexpected something is the
more you will learn about it."[4]

So if you want your man to remember you, to learn more about
you, surprise—or wow—him! What would catch your husband off
guard? What activity does he least expect you to do with him or for
him (outside the bedroom)?

Wow Wisdom

Your second assignment is to ask your husband, "What would wow you inside the bedroom?" Then listen. Tell your husband that this is a brainstorming session, and some of the ideas might happen but some might not. This gives you the freedom to surprise him by keeping things exciting and unpredictable, and it also gives you freedom to stay within your sexual preference parameters.

This conversation may help get you in the mood too. If this is a stretch for you, simply pray, *Lord, give me the want to, to want to have sex with my man.* Soon you will find yourself saying,

> How handsome you are, my beloved!
> Oh, how charming!
> And our bed is verdant.
> (Song of Solomon 1:16)

Wow Date

When I speak to women about how to have a red-hot relationship, I also encourage the element of surprise in a way that stimulates the sensory part of the brain. If you want a truly memorable date, you want to create an experience, so incorporate all five senses: touch, taste, smell, sound, and sight.

Become a detective and over the next few days, and far apart from each other, make note of the answers to questions like:

- Honey, what is your favorite scent? (smell)
- What kind of music would you like to listen to tonight in the car? (sound)
- Family dinner question, "Everyone name their three favorite comfort foods." (taste)
- If you had to pick one article of clothing out of my closet by touch, which item would you love the texture of most? (touch)
- Sweetie, when we are on vacation, what would you like to see? (sight)

Now see if you can weave together a memorable date by surprising him with the unexpected activity outside the bedroom first, then intertwine all his favorites behind those bedroom doors as the unanticipated dessert. To make it truly a surprise, wait until he has forgotten you asked any of these questions!

Wow 10

Heart Healthy

Sometimes wowing your man is more of a challenge as tough circumstances come crashing down around his life. The death of a child, a health issue, a financial setback, or caring for an ill family member can bring overwhelming heartbreak. One couple that knows this pain is Carol and Gene Kent, whose only son is currently incarcerated with a life sentence. Carol, best-selling author of *When I Lay My Isaac Down, A New Kind of Normal,* and *Between a Rock and a Grace Place,* now has a love that feels surrounded by the razor wire of Hardee Correctional Facility.

Wow Assignment

As you look at your husband's life, look with eyes of empathy and sympathy:

- Sympathy is feeling sorrow *for* your mate. You pity him.
- Empathy is feeling sorrow *with* your mate. You are pained with him.

What would lift his spirits? Look for a way to not just placate your spouse, but go the extra mile and pay tribute to him and his strength in a meaningful way.

Wow Wisdom

Carol writes:

> From the time J.P. was a child, Gene read to our son. He read all seven books in *The Chronicles of Narnia* to J.P. out loud. Aslan, the Lion, was always a favorite character because he symbolized God in all of His remarkable power, love, compassion, and peace.
>
> I was speaking in Columbus, Georgia, last year and walked into an antique shop. There it was—a small brass sculpture of a lion with a flowing mane, lying on a book. On the card to Gene, I wrote:
>
>> Dear Gene,
>>
>> This gift is a reminder of the incredible father you were to J.P. during his growing up years, and of the father you are today in the middle of more challenging circumstances.
>>
>> This lion reminds me that our God is still in control!
>>
>> Love,
>> Carol

Sometimes we women forget men experience deep emotional pain too. King David cried out to God, "Return, Lord, and deliver me" (Psalm 6:4), and again in Psalm 31:2 he exclaims,

> Turn your ear to me,
>   come quickly to my rescue;
> be my rock of refuge,
>   a strong fortress to save me.

If the king with all the resources of the nation at his fingertips cried out for rescue, our man might on occasion feel the need for a life preserver too. In a world that can make a man feel tossed overboard in a stormy sea, we can reflect the nature of Jesus, who in Galatians 1:4 is described as one "who gave himself for our sins to *rescue* us from the present evil age."

In one particularly painful season of ministry for Bill, I sensed his need for rescue. Simply being in the same city where the ministry upheaval happened pained him greatly, so I whisked him away to one of the spots in the mountains where I knew he had always found peace and solace in the past.

Wow Date

Even in life's painful moments, you as a wife can ease the burden by looking for ways to alleviate and rescue, even for a moment, the heaviness of your mate's heart. Carol describes one way she did this:

> Gene has always loved musical theater, but ever since our son's arrest and conviction for murder, we spend every at-home Saturday and Sunday in the prison visitation room, so doing "fun" things on weekends is more rare than it used to be. Gene's birthday was coming up and it fell on a Sunday. As we left the prison and walked to the parking lot, I announced: "We're not going home yet. We're headed to Tampa."
>
> I surprised him with a lovely dinner out at his favorite restaurant, followed by an evening at the theater where we saw the Broadway production of *The Lion King*. For a few hours we escaped into a fantasy of fun, frivolity, and togetherness in a joy-filled atmosphere.
>
> Later he said: "Today meant a lot to me. Thank you for making my birthday special and for planning a memory-making getaway."

Now it's your turn. What will lift the heaviness from your husband's shoulders, even for a few hours?

The Flavor of Intimacy

One of our favorite dates over our thirty-plus years together is to walk or bike to our local ice cream shop. Behind the glass are so many choices, and we drool as we scan flavors like Quarterback Crunch, Jamoca Almond Fudge, Love Potion #31, Cotton Candy, Chocolate Mousse Royale, and Super Fudge Truffle. Or if we're feeling a bit more health conscious, we might stand in the mile-long line outside the famous Yogurt Mill in our hometown of El Cajon, California, and choose something good for us like a nonfat yogurt with fresh fruit. Yes, we all *love* our choices.

Wow Assignment

Some choices serve as prerequisites. In school, to get into the upper-division courses we were most interested in, we had to pass basic courses in English, math, and some kind of science. In the same way, if we truly want a sex life that sizzles, we need to make sure all our love prerequisites are taken care of. In *Red-Hot Monogamy*, Bill and I created an eight-week guidebook to turn up the temperature in the bedroom. We contend that intimacy is being on the same page in eight vital areas:

- Social
- Financial
- Recreational
- Vocational
- Parental
- Emotional
- Spiritual
- Sexual

If you have intimacy in the first seven, chances are it will be much easier for you and your mate to have intimacy sexually too.

Wow Wisdom

Look at the list above and review which area has been the cause of your most recent arguments or conflicts. If your husband can't trust the way you spend (or resist saving) money, he might not feel very amorous toward you. Or if you are in constant disagreement on how best to raise the kids, things will soon cool off behind the bedroom door.

Begin praying for your marriage in this area of contention. Research books, conferences, classes, and mentors who could help you make headway in this tense area. Own the issue from *your* side of the equation. As your spouse sees you improve in areas he has been frustrated with you, his heart will be drawn toward yours—and toward your body! (He might get motivated to own his side of the equation too.)

Wow Date

Find a creative way to give the news of this small change as a gift to your mate. If you've had conflict with your finances, use coupons to save on groceries, then take the savings and get something your husband has been longing to own. Wrap the gift in your grocery receipts so your husband can enjoy his new gift with no guilt!

Or if the area of conflict is vocational growth, maybe the small change is getting up to make breakfast for your man before he leaves for work or getting home to greet him as he enters, or deciding to commute together one day a week to gain more couple time.

If a social or recreational change is needed, maybe accompany him to that business dinner or cancel one of your social engagements to create another night at home with your spouse. This small sacrifice just might pay big dividends.

It's your choice!

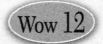
Wow 12

A New Pattern for Love

My friend Carole Lewis, national director of First Place 4Health, has been happily married for over fifty-one years, so she is an expert on wowing her man. She shares one of those powerful keys to long-lasting love:

> There was never a fuss made over special occasions when my husband, Johnny, was growing up. The four boys never had a birthday party and each boy received one present at Christmas…
>
> The year that Johnny turned forty, I wanted to really blow his socks off to make him feel loved and special. I decided that I would buy him a beautiful ring that would let him know, every time he looked at it, how special he is to me…
>
> When he opened the box, his eyes lit up like a child receiving their first bike. Johnny turned forty in 1979 and to this day, that ring is the only possession he is afraid of losing (except for me, of course).

Wow Assignment

What special celebrations or rituals did your husband miss out on as a kid? How can you celebrate that special occasion with him this year? For example, because my husband's mother struggles with mental illness, his life was very isolated. He never attended summer camp or family reunions, and they never experienced things like backyard barbeques or in-home parties for fun things like the Super Bowl or July 4. Because of this, all our married life I have gone out of my way to provide these experiences for Bill.

Wow Wisdom

In Carole's book, *A Thankful Heart,* she writes about how to break a harmful pattern from our past.

> Chances are, you didn't receive something you needed from certain family members, and you've wasted a lot of time trying to receive that particular something from these people (who may not have a clue about your need). I strongly believe you can break that pattern by reversing the trend. We can get what we've missed, not by grasping or clutching from these people, but by giving to them…
>
> I'm talking about the type of lavish giving that expects nothing in return. If we begin giving our spouses the admiration, encouragement and unconditional love they perhaps didn't receive from their parents, God will begin healing our marriage.[5]

Wow Date

Cami's husband always wanted a pony as a kid, so she took him horseback riding.

Sandy's man had to quit college in order to care for his single mom with cancer, so Sandy saved up her earnings to give her husband one semester of college on her dime.

Trina's husband was raised by a vegan mom who also didn't believe in sugar or sweets, so Trina barbequed some ribs and baked her spouse his favorite chocolate cake.

What would you like to do with or for your man to wow him? Turn his pain into a party in his honor.

Bank on It

Men joke about the cost of having a wife:

- *Joint checking account:* a handy little device that permits my wife to beat me to the draw.

- "The husband who wants a happy marriage should learn to keep his mouth shut and his checkbook open."
  —Groucho Marx

- "There's a way of transferring funds that is even faster than electronic banking. It's called marriage."—James Holt McGavran

- A man said his credit card was stolen, but he decided not to report it since the thief was spending much less than his wife did.

- A woman told her friend, "I made my husband a millionaire."

  "And what was he before you married him?" asked the friend.

  "A billionaire."

Wow Assignment

Money problems in marriage are not the real problem, just a symptom of the real issue: our motivation in life. Here are four main inner drives or motivations:[6]

Inner Drive 1: Authority—For those who are motivated by having authority, money is power. People motivated in this way are highly productive, visionary, focused, and hard-working. They have the capacity to handle large budgets and large challenges and take large risks. With spiritual depth, they can accomplish much for a family. However, the pursuit can cause them to let others slip down their priority list. One solution might be to set aside a certain amount each month toward the dreamer's long-term goal while a stable amount is used for family needs.

Inner Drive 2: Attention—Money makes memories. Money is all about people. As a result, people motivated by this inner drive are very generous; they will give you the shirt off their back. Your family finances work out easier if this person is given the freedom to work hard to earn extra money that is set aside as discretionary funds. For the spouse married to the generous heart, create a discretionary amount he or she can spend without consulting you.

Inner Drive 3: Acceptance—This person purchases peace. The goal is to create as simple a process as possible toward money. If the family is spending less than it makes, this person relaxes. If, however, more is being spent than earned, the result is stress. These people remind us that life is not all about money. You will find your marriage is better when you commit to a savings account for peace of mind.

Inner Drive 4: Accuracy—This person is all about following a system, and they are emotionally attached to a budget. They take the budget literally, so if the budget says $50 for groceries per week, they mean $50—not $55. They are savers and planners. The key to working things out with someone motivated in this way is to discuss ahead of time any variations from the plan.

Wow Wisdom

Your husband's motivation style might be very different from yours, but this shouldn't be looked at as a negative. The Bible reminds us that "as iron sharpens iron, so one person sharpens another" (Proverbs 27:17). I like to put a feminine twist on this idea by reminding myself that the best way to cut and polish a diamond is with another diamond.[7] His differences, even in this area, can make you a better person.

Wow Date

This date can be practical, like discussing the family budget, your money motivation styles, or completing the "Motivational Budget" found in *The Marriage Code*.[8] Or strengthen your skills with money with a resource like *A Woman's Guide to Family Finance* by Ellie Kay, then share with your mate what you have learned. The point of the date is not just to make headway in the area of finances but to think of a way to thank your man for his unique motivational style and his way of interacting with money—and with you.

Wow 14

Money Make Up

Dear Jack,

My amazing man, I am lost without you. I have been going crazy since I broke off our engagement. I think I must have lost my mind. Won't you please consider coming back to me? There will never be another man like you. No one can ever hold a candle to you. I can never marry another man quite like you. I need you. My world is just not the same without you in it. Please forgive me and let's try again. Love you like there is no tomorrow.

Forever yours,

Jill

P.S. Congrats! I hear you won the lottery.

Okay, it's just a joke! But disagreements over money are no laughing matter. According to a Utah State University study, "Couples who reported disagreeing about finance once a week were over 30 percent more likely to get divorced."[9] And plenty of couples fight this often over money. "Money is the number one thing that couples fight about in America," says Howard Markman, professor of psychology and director of the Center for Marital and Family Studies at the University of Denver. "Since financial decisions have to be made almost daily, it's a frequent source of disagreement."[10]

Wow Assignment

When my son was dating Hannah, the girl who is now his wife, he was raving to me about her many wonderful qualities: her beauty, her wit and humor, her brains, her spiritual depth. Then he added with a smile, "And she even likes to save money. She's like a coupon queen. Mom, she's amazing!" My reply was "Marry the girl!"

Make him glad he married you by looking at the checkbook through his eyes. Maybe he is motivated by authority and his bravery has launched your family into new adventures. Or perhaps his warm heart funds plenty of memories for family and friends. Maybe his desire for a savings account "just in case" has rescued you a time or two. Or his dedication to the details of the budget may have carved out some extra money for that long-hoped-for vacation.

Wow Wisdom

Be brave and pray this for yourself: *Lord, help me see my husband's view of life and money from Your point of view, a gift to me and our family. Amen.*

Wow Date

Find a way to creatively thank your spouse for the way he sees and handles the family funds. It could be as simple as sticking to that budget he's set up or trying things his way without complaining.

But you might want to go that extra mile and write a thank-you note and tuck it in a money clip. You could even set aside some of your funds and then surprise him with a gift he has hoped for or match some of his funds so together you can reach one of your special goals. If he is the main breadwinner, do something that says, "Thanks! I notice all your hard work on our behalf." If you are the primary provider, look for a way to honor his contribution to your family's success.

Wow 15

Every Day Counts

As a professor I taught during the day and did research at night. I would usually take a break around nine, however, calling up my favorite strategy game on the Internet and playing with an online team. One night I was paired with a veteran of the game who was a master strategist...after six games we were undefeated. Suddenly, my fearless leader informed me his mom wanted him to go to bed.

"How old are you?" I typed.

"Twelve," he replied. "How old are you?"

Feeling my face redden, I answered, "Eight."

A man's got to have some downtime. One of my friends routinely complained that her husband spent altogether too much time in his recliner watching football. One morning she found her mate collapsed, called for help, and then held him as he died in her arms. She said to me, "I'd give anything to see him sitting in that old recliner again."

Wow Assignment

Figure out how long you might have left with your mate. Most people will live into their seventies,[11] but some of us will unfortunately become widows before then. The median age for all women in the U.S. today is thirty-six, and the median age for widows is fifty-seven.[12] That means the typical woman in this country may have just over a thousand more Saturdays with her mate. Wouldn't it be nice to have a few more? Do your own countdown. If you become a widow at today's median age, how many more days might you have with your spouse?

Wow Wisdom

You might add a few years to your husband's life because you allow him time to decompress. Isn't that a nice investment? Plus, you will feel great about the memories you have with him. You'll be able to recollect happy, precious, relaxed snapshots of time instead of all the nagging, bossing, or whining to get him to do your list of chores.

Sure, the basics of life need to be handled, but honestly ask yourself how many of the things on your honey-do list are really needs and how many can wait or at least be paced out? Even God rested! "By the seventh day God had finished the work he had been doing; so on the seventh day he rested from all his work" (Genesis 2:2).

Wow Date

Thank God that your man is here to enjoy today. Tell your husband you are grateful, thankful, and happy to have him around—then play hooky. Take the day off with your guy. Let him pick the activity, and drop the to-do list and go have fun. Have a party for two in a field, tube the river, or go swimming while the kids are in school.

Be Willing

I heard about a man who just wouldn't give in and go see a doctor for his aches and pains. (This resistance to medical attention is a common male trait.) The story goes like this:

> Following a storm, my husband worked long hours clearing the jumble of trees that littered our property. The longer he worked, the more painful it became for him to move his right arm. He ignored my pleas to see the doctor until one night he yelped, "Ow! This is getting serious." As I turned to him in concern, he added, "Now it hurts to push buttons on the remote!"

If he'd just be willing! Willing to accept help, willing to listen to your wisdom, willing to admit when he's wrong, willing to go along with your plan. We all love it when our husband has a willing heart, but how willing is your heart?

Wow Assignment

Make note of your own stubborn streak. I have seen wives argue with their husband over nonissues, like:

- "Why didn't you turn left here? I would have."
- "Here, give me the baby. That's not the way that outfit is supposed to be."
- "Let me butter the toast. You always put too much on."

We women can nitpick our men to death. This week make note of your own unwillingness—your own resistance.

Wow Wisdom

Pray for a willing heart. Live a little on the edge by being spontaneous and open to new ideas that didn't originate with you. The ability to have a willing heart is about trusting your spouse, but even more so, a willing heart shows you trust God. You believe God is big enough, powerful enough, cares and loves you enough to lead you *through* your husband, not just through you. Today, pray for yourself, that you will gain a willing heart, a heart ready to say, "Yes, Dear!"

Wow Date

Does it really matter if he takes his way or your way to church—as long as you get to church? It is better to get there more in love, not less in love than when you left home. Plan a date where all you do is ask questions of your mate and do the date his way. The conversation might look like one fork in the road after another, with your husband picking the path each time:

"Honey, would you like to do something active or watch a movie? A movie? Super. Action, drama, or comedy? Drama? You pick. Thanks, honey! Looking forward to our time together."

Wow 17

The Fig Leaf

I blame Eve. I mean there she was in the garden with a good man, in a good place, and a good plan. After God created man and woman, He said: "Be fruitful and increase in number [have red-hot monogamy]; fill the earth and subdue it." *(Total dominion as a couple. Nice.)*

"Then God said, 'I give you every seed-bearing plant on the face of the whole earth and every tree that has fruit with seed in it. They will be yours for food. And to all the beasts of the earth and all the birds in the sky and all the creatures that move along the ground...I give every green plant for food.'" *(God supplied the food. No grocery shopping. Awesome!)*

"God saw all that he had made, and it was very good" (Genesis 1:28-31). *(I ditto God—very good!)*

Wow Assignment

There was just one rule in Eden: "You are free to eat from any tree in the garden; but you must not eat from the tree of the knowledge of good and evil, for when you eat from it you will certainly die" (Genesis 2:16-17).

Okay Eve, what part of "must not eat" and "certainly die" did you not get? Eve, you have made my life and the lives of all wives harder. We all have that same "well, that's a nice plan, God, but let me help ya out a bit" attitude.

This week, make note of how often you want life to run on *your* plan.

Wow Wisdom

The thing we girls fight is the need to control. You don't always have to be in the driver's seat. No one died and made you God. Kill the control freak inside! You do not always have to be right. Life doesn't have to be lived just *your* way. Practice the prayer that even Jesus prayed: "Not my will but yours be done" (Luke 2:42).

Wow Date

Take it back to Eden. One of my friends had the right "Eden-like" idea: "On our anniversary at a state parks cabin, I tied a big ribbon around myself while wearing my birthday suit. Needless to say, my husband loved his present!"

Another friend rented a beach house with an outdoor shower with smoked-glass sides but that opened to the sky. She and her husband took more showers together that vacation week than they ever had before!

A neighbor put in a Jacuzzi with a jungle's worth of plant screens and added a bed with no roof for lovemaking under the stars.

How can you get your husband back to Eden?

Wow 18

Yes, Dear

I married Miss Right. I just didn't know her first name was Always." Because I am a firstborn, I was trained to be bossy. Opinions come easy to me, and I have to deliberately decide to defer. I don't think I'm alone in this either. Plenty of women who are not firstborn also have a hard time holding back the urge to get in the last word or put in their two cents. One joke puts it this way:

> Two husbands were discussing their married lives. Although happily married, they admitted that there were arguments sometimes.
>
> "I've made one great discovery," Chad said. "I know how to always have the last word."
>
> "Wow!" Sherman said. "How did you manage that?"
>
> "It's easy. My last word is always 'Yes, Dear.'"[13]

Wow Assignment

Try turning that around. This week, you try saying, "Yes, Dear" without rolling your eyes or being sarcastic. (I know. I've been tempted too.)

I'm not saying don't have an opinion. I don't think for most women there's much chance of falling off that end of the scale! But I am asking you to find or create some areas where you'd be willing to trust your husband's leadership and do things his way and not give your opinion.

Of all the varied opinions you express, how many are truly high-impact areas, things that really affect you, your future, and your ability to succeed? On the other hand, how many more are simply preferences and desires?

Wow Wisdom

Perhaps you should try to release a little at a time—you can do it. Really, you can! On minor issues, I try to withhold an opinion and instead simply say a version of "Yes, Dear":

- "Sounds good."
- "Nice plan."
- "Appreciate your diligence on this."
- "Great idea!"
- "Let's run with that."
- "Thanks for thinking this through for us."

Wow Date

"Yes, Dear" is usually a great way to hold your tongue. Things might not have been done your way, but it is *God's way* to be willing to follow your husband's lead.

This week plan a "Yes, Dear" date. Create a "Yes!" atmosphere by doing a few things you might normally say no to. Say yes to hunting, fishing, running, going to the computer store, lumberyard, or livestock auction. Wherever you normally would say no, replace that response with, "Yes, Dear!"

Say yes this week to as many things as you can by trusting God for the outcome. Release the reins and allow your husband to lead. You might need to start small, so practice it now by saying out loud, "Yes, Dear!"

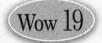

Sure, Why Not?

At one marriage conference we spoke at, the pastor surveyed the men on what they perceived as "intimacy." The survey results began with "The man could use some silence!" But the top vote was, "Walk around the house buck naked."

So let's just say it. Sometimes what will wow your man is a little bit of adventure in your sexual life.

One of my best friends forever said, "When we have gone out of town on business or for a getaway, he's always asked me to 'bring a little something.' On one occasion, not wanting to spend money on what spends most of its life in the back of my drawer, I brought all of my old lingerie and gave him a personal fashion show. He talked about it for years!"

Wow Assignment

Our book *Red-Hot Monogamy* has two hundred red-hot ideas for adding spice and sizzle to your sex life. At the end of each chapter is a section we call "Hands-on Homework" (pun completely intended). This is homework he will want to do! It also contains some provocative questions so you can know what's really going on in your man's heart and mind when it comes to his sexual hopes and desires. Be bold. Ask your man one of these questions from our book:

- If my hands are placed over your eyes and I said, "Surprise!" what would you want to see when you opened your eyes?
- What part of your body do you most enjoy me touching?
- What kind of light is sexiest to you for lovemaking: full sunshine outdoors, lights on in our room or daylight, candlelight or Christmas lights, or complete darkness?
- What smell or taste is an aphrodisiac to you to help you get in the mood?
- What sound (music or other sound) makes you want to make love?
- What do you like me to wear (or not) that helps you want to make love to me?

Wow Wisdom

In *The 10 Best Decisions a Couple Can Make,* we have a chapter on sex that lists three gifts to create red-hot romance. One of those gifts is the gift of adventure. The idea of adventure is from Solomon's wife, who proclaimed "our bed is verdant" (Song of Solomon 1:16). *Verdant* is not a word we hear or use often. It literally means *green* or *lush,* and it may indicate that the couple is outdoors. She thinks their love life is flourishing, thriving, and lush, and it could be taken as a hint she would be open to lovemaking in an oasis setting—outdoors. That is adventurous!

Wow Date

Solomon's bride invited her man to a two-sided sexual wow:

Let us go early to the vineyards
   to see if the vines have budded,

if their blossoms have opened,
>   and if the pomegranates are in bloom—
>   there I will give you my love.
The mandrakes send out their fragrance,
>   and at our door is every delicacy,
both new and old,
>   that I have stored up for you, my beloved.

(Song of Solomon 7:12-13)

She invited her man out to the vineyard for some lovemaking and said it would be something old (we've done before) and something new (something he has wanted to try). This is definitely an adventurous invitation.

Think of your own adventure your guy might enjoy. Perhaps something old and something new?

Wow 20

Own Your Issue

In *Overcoming the Dark Side of Leadership,* Gary MacIntosh and Samuel Rima expose us to the reality that we all have issues. I have condensed their material dramatically, given it a feminine twist and my own application to give a snapshot of what baggage you might be carrying that can negatively impact your love life. (I highly recommend you read *Overcoming the Dark Side of Leadership* and take the test inside the book.)

Wow Assignment

All of us have tendencies toward unhealthy behavior. Which of the following best describes you?

Compulsive: She is status conscious, exercises authority or looks for approval from authority, and is controlling or a workaholic. Productivity and approval reassure her. She can also be moralistic or judgmental. Let me illustrate with a sentence for each dark side:

I do and will sacrifice sleep, time with my spouse, or other priorities to get it done so I get applause or approval.

Narcissistic: She believes life should revolve around her, her needs, her ideas. She is driven to succeed by a need for admiration or acclaim. Deep down she feels insecure and inferior, so she needs to build herself up.

I do because I believe my way is the best way. I only want to do my plan and want you to applaud and cheer my plan.

Paranoid: Her fears stop her from living a normal life. She is suspicious, jealous, fearful, and hypersensitive. She fears others might do something to unravel her. She attaches subjective meanings to others' motives and can create rigid structures to maintain control of situations or people.

I don't do because I am afraid of what might happen if I did.

Codependent: She seeks approval from a toxic person or lives life around another's needs and desires to the detriment of her own life or needs. She does not want to confront real issues but would rather cover them up. She takes on others' work and burdens and is repressed or frustrated because she never speaks her true feelings.

I do and I hope you approve of what I do, yet I am mad because you are not helping me do it.

Passive-Aggressive: She establishes one expectation then does the opposite. She is stubborn, intentionally inefficient, lazy, or forgetful. She complains, resists, and procrastinates as a means of controlling others.

I will say I will do it, but I will decide when or if I will really do it.

Wow Wisdom

Did you resist the temptation to try to identify your husband's baggage? It's easy for us to identify the flaws in our mate and ignore the baggage we carry that might be negatively affecting our love. The psalmist prayed "see if there is any offensive way in me" (Psalm 139:24).

Wow Date

Plan a date where you own your issue, and then make a step to make amends:

Compulsive? Then drop your to-do list and spontaneously whisk your mate away for something fun.

Narcissistic? Then make a red-carpet date with your mate as the center of attention.

Paranoid? Face down a fear and do something your husband knows you are usually afraid to do.

Codependent? Speak your heart and plan and implement a date of *your* dreams, and invite your mate into your fantasy experience.

Passive-Aggressive? Step up and carry through with a date plan your husband knows you've been dragging your feet on.

Wow 21

The Unexpected

Surprise. Many men love that word because it means things have not become stale or routine. So astonish, astound, amaze, flabbergast, stun, and blow away that husband of yours and plan a big surprise!

Wow Assignment

To wow your man you need some information, so put on that thinking cap:

- What is his lifelong dream?
- What or who does he love watching on TV?
- Where are those special places from his past?
- Where has he always hoped to go?
- What activity replenishes him most?
- Where has he wanted to have red-hot monogamy?

Wow Wisdom

God loves to give surprises too. Just think of the Christmas story when the angels announced Christ's birth: "And an angel of the Lord *suddenly* stood before them, and the glory of the Lord shone around them…And *suddenly* there appeared with the angel a multitude of the heavenly host praising God" (Luke 2:9,13 NASB).

Or the Easter story when angels proclaim Jesus' resurrection:

> On the first day of the week, very early in the morning, the women took the spices they had prepared and went to the tomb. They found the stone rolled away from the tomb, but when they entered, they did not find the body of the Lord Jesus. While they were wondering about this, *suddenly* two men in clothes that gleamed like lightning stood beside them…the men said to them, "He is not here; he has risen!" (Luke 24:1-6).

Wow Date

The most important part of the surprise is the invitation. Here are a few ideas from some of my friends that really wowed their husbands:

- I sprinkled red silk hearts all over his desk and office. There was also a note on his desk indicating my intentions for the evening.

- On our fifteenth wedding anniversary, I told my hubby I wanted to eat at a special restaurant in San Diego. During dessert, I excused myself to go to the powder room. The maître d' then came over to my husband and said, "The lady left this card for you." Inside was a key to a hotel room. (I had driven down earlier in the day and booked and prepared the room.) When he entered the room, he found me and lots of rose petals on the bed. He loved the surprise!

- While hiking in the Hawaiian jungle, I pulled my husband to the ground in a "Me Jane–You Tarzan" way. After twenty years of marriage, I am sure it caught him by surprise. Red-hot monogamy in the Garden of Eden must have made Adam happy too.

- I tied a hotel key to the string of a Mylar balloon and tucked it into his briefcase. When he opened his case in the middle of a business meeting, he was surprised with the good news of a wife waiting for him. Funny, he didn't really care if he landed that business deal after he opened his briefcase.

- When I was employed as a producer for a local TV station, I used to get all kinds of perks. On one occasion, a new hotel-casino was opening up, and I was given a free room for the festivities. I decided to make a romantic date night out of it. I booked the room without telling my husband. Then, on the day of the reservation, I packed our suitcases full of goodies and put them in the car. When he came home from work, I presented him with a handmade card that read, "You are cordially invited to attend a surprise getaway with your wife at the so-and-so casino resort. Even if you don't gamble a penny, you are *guaranteed* to get lucky! Your ride leaves in 10 minutes. Just bring your smile." Let me tell you, it was a great evening, even if we never did make it to the official festivities at the hotel!

Wow 22

Get a Pen

My friend K!mberly shares how picking up a pen helped her create a long-lasting love to look forward to:

> In the fall of 2008...my journal turned into one long chronicle of a pity party. Among other physical issues, I was having a minute-by-minute losing battle with "taking every negative thought captive" and was diagnosed with depression.
>
> One of the antidotes for this was starting an exercise of "choosing joy." I...made a pact with myself that every day I'd write only the highlight, or even multiple highlights, of each day. When I look back on this year, I don't want to remember any of the doctor visits, disappointments, frustrations of living abroad, or just living. I want to remember the good...It's becoming a little treasure book...God has new things for me. Scripture says his mercies are new every morning. With this joy journal, I'm keeping track of them.[14]

Wow Assignment

Now it's your turn. Buy a small calendar or journal and keep track of the good things God sends along your path. Dr. Robert A. Emmons, in his book *Thanks! How the New Science of Gratitude Can Make You Happier*, shares the results of a study that shows just being grateful raises your happiness level by 25 percent.[15] Your grandma's wisdom to "count your many blessings" is a key element in finding and keeping personal joy and happiness. Bill and I have taken turns listing alphabetically traits we value in each other, and we have penned lists of reasons why we are grateful for each other and we keep those lists posted inside our desk as reminders of why we love each other (which is especially helpful on those days you don't *feel* like wowing your man).

Wow Wisdom

K!mberly writes,

> At the end of every week, I pick the highlight of the week and put it in red pen over the week. Verses from Scripture that have significance also make it in red, along with any other insights I hear or have about what a joy it is to be alive and called by God...The theme of my year has become "His strength is made perfect in my weakness," as day after day, week after week, I get tangible evidence of Jesus' mercies.[16]

Wow Date

Tonight, count the blessing of your man. Do as Solomon's wife did and list off the things you admire about his body (Song of Solomon 5:10-16). Do as the psalmist and list off, A to Z, the best traits of your guy.[17] Or for each year you've been married, recount a highlight, something you loved to do with him.

Set aside a date to take your husband out and share your joy journal with him, then re-create a few bedroom memories. Do something that would make him write in his joy journal!

Creatures of Habit

Author Madeleine L'Engle says, "Sometimes idiosyncrasies which used to be irritating become endearing, part of the complexity of a partner who has become woven deep into our own selves."[18]

How about your honey? Which of his idiosyncrasies drive you nuts? One of my friends had a husband who loved fixing up old cars, so car parts packed their garage and yard. It was his only vice. He was a great community leader, father, church leader, and husband—all except those crazy car parts! So she decided a good man with unwelcome car-part collectibles was better than no man or a bad man. Good choice. She dug in and learned about antique cars, how to find deals on car parts, went on dates with him to car shows—and you know what? Eventually those parts became a real car—one they can date in!

Wow Assignment

Now it's your turn. Make a list of some of the small irritations, annoying habits, and idiosyncrasies of your man. Then next to each irritation, write out the upside or why you can choose to love that part of who he is. Here are a few examples:

It drives me crazy when…	*But I can love that because…*
he runs late all the time.	he is a good listener and cares for people.
he spends money on tools.	he is handy around the house.
he is such a sports fanatic.	his enthusiasm and loyalty are admirable.

Wow Wisdom

Turn that irritation inside out. The Bible puts it this way: "Be gentle and forbearing with one another and, if one has a difference (a grievance or complaint) against another, readily pardoning each other" (Colossians 3:13 AMP).

Wow Date

Make a big deal out of one of the small irritations you have with your mate. Turn the negative into a positive. Study your man's idiosyncrasies and annoying habits and see if any can be redeemed and turned into a gift to warm his heart and brighten his day:

- If he is a sports superfan, buy a jersey of his favorite team and use it for your pj's.
- If he is a fishing nut, grab a rod and reel and take him to a little cabin in the back woods.
- If he is a car enthusiast, rent a sports car and head down a scenic highway.
- If he is a computer geek, camp out in line with him at midnight for that next new edition of Microsoft whatever—but bring comfy chairs, food, and music to pass the time.

Make this a frequent prayer: *Lord, help me turn those small annoyances into big ways to creatively love my man. Amen.* Surprise him with a little taste of what he loves and maybe, just maybe, you might start loving it too.

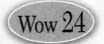

Wow 24

His Point of View

While researching this book, I asked some of our guy pals what they perceived as romantic. It's much more than the stereotypical, "Take me to the bedroom." Sometimes it's listening in a way that takes action. Our friend Gene Kent explains it from a male point of view:

During most of our marriage, I've begged and encouraged Carol to do some exercise with me, but to no avail. In January 2009, she went to a health retreat with several of her speaker and author friends. She was there for a week and her calls home seemed to be more energetic than usual. She was having a great time recharging her spirit.

When I picked her up at the airport, she wanted to go immediately to a sports apparel store. She said the emphasis at the retreat was on being physically fit as well as spiritually fit, and she was convicted about not making exercise a priority. The retreat emphasized how a healthy lifestyle meant she'd have more years to have a more energetic, rewarding, and longer life together with the man she loved. She had begun walking several miles a day while at the retreat and was determined to do that on every at-home day.

That was eighteen months ago, twenty-five pounds ago, and hundreds of miles ago. Walking four miles a day is now a habit we do together nearly every day. We walk and pray for our son, our future, our friends, and our ministry. I am still wowed and surprised with her change of heart.

Wow Assignment

What has your husband been bugging you to do? What event, hobby, or responsibility is he secretly—or openly—hoping you will be a part of? Do you know he wants you to take a day off, take better care of your health, join him at an activity, but you always find a reason to put him off or procrastinate?

Wow Wisdom

Listening to God is a verb. The book of James explains, "But someone will say, 'You have faith; I have deeds.' Show me your faith without deeds, and I will show you my faith by my deeds" (James 2:18). In the same way, your actions will speak louder than your words to your man.

Wow Date

Make a date to trade in your point of view (POV) for his POV. If you're a workaholic, invite him out and give him a new calendar marking the nights off with him. If you're a social butterfly and he's a homebody, wrap up the TV remote with some popcorn or a video. If you're messy and he's a neatnik, clean out that closet that's driving him crazy.

Wow 25

Addicted to Hubby

What if we were as in love with our husband as some people are with their coffee or other addictive substances? You know you are addicted to coffee if...

You grind your coffee beans in your mouth.

You sleep with your eyes open.

The only time you're standing still is during an earthquake.

You can jump-start your car without cables.

You walk twenty miles on your treadmill before you realize it's not plugged in.

Instant coffee takes too long.

You have a picture of your coffee mug on your coffee mug.[19]

There can be an upside to coffee addiction. Coffee does keep you more alert when driving.[20] Java helps you work or exercise longer.[21] And WebMD cites studies that show a cup of joe can lower the risk of Parkinson's and diabetes.[22] "There's also some evidence that coffee may help manage asthma and even control attacks when medication is unavailable, stop a headache, boost mood, and even prevent cavities."[23]

Wow Assignment

Think what your life would be like if you needed your husband as much as you need coffee. You'd wake up looking forward to holding him. You'd race to the kitchen to find him. You'd visit him several times a day. You'd look for new ways to enjoy him. You'd tell everyone about his best qualities. Yes, our marriages might be better if we treated our husband with the respect and attention we give our coffee mugs.

I know what a coffee lover looks like; I live with one. So embrace your husband more than you might embrace your java. Love him more than you love your freshly ground and roasted brew.

Wow Wisdom

I like this picture of positively addicting love: "Above all, keep fervent in your love for one another" (1 Peter 4:8 NASB). *Fervent* means to love unconditionally "with effort and consistency." This is a love that's leaning in, leaning forward—a love that's looking for ways to keep loving bigger, stronger, and better. Fervent love is the kind that looks forward to "the workout" and longs for the next opportunity to give itself away. Ask God to show you how to fervently love your man.

Wow Date

When people become friends with my husband, Bill, they often send him coffee mugs with cute or clever sayings such as:

- Instant Human, Just Add Coffee
- Coffee and Love Taste Best When Hot
- Sleep Is a Symptom of Caffeine Deprivation
- Coffee lover seeking BREAK from usual GRIND[24]

Our sons have added to the collection with mugs from their universities, the high schools where they coach, or events they compete in. Those mugs sit on a special shelf because they are valued enough to protect.

This week, show your man you value him enough to protect his life and do something that shows "I can't live without you." Love him more than your coffee, chocolate, designer bag, or a spa day. This week, share some of your favorite indulgences with him. Draw him a hot bath, share your dark chocolate, and yes, if you both like coffee, share a cup of gourmet blend together.

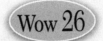

His Essence

In the book *Eat, Pray, Love,* which later became a blockbuster movie, the main character is in search of herself, and is given an assignment to find a word that is the essence of who she is. Not *writer* or *girlfriend,* which describes what she does or a role she has. Rather, she is challenged to describe what is in the core of who she is, the way God created her.

Most women reading the book likely felt compelled to discover *their* word, the essence of *themselves*. Instead, I looked over at my husband, and a rush of fondness, admiration, and sweet emotion hit me as a flood. My heart actually beat so hard, I thought I was having a heart attack! I love, adore, am drawn to Bill like a magnet, because of the essence of my amazing man.

Wow Assignment

At that moment of heart arrhythmia, I prayed, *Lord, show me the essence of Bill in a fresh way.* I began to list off in my mind several descriptive words:

- Kind
- Wise

- Patient
- Caring
- Manly
- Gorgeous
- Positive

As I narrowed the field, *wise* and *kind* seemed to be the front runners. Then it hit me and I smiled. We had just completed the process of branding our life's work and giving our ministry a new name: Love-Wise. That is really the essence of Bill. He isn't just kind, he oozes 1 Corinthians 13, "the love chapter." And everyone, I mean everyone, continually compliments him on his insightful wisdom. Bill is where love and wisdom intersect. He is that dash between Love and Wise.

Now you try it. Ask God to show you the essence of your man. What one word (or two) would you use to sum him up?

Wow Wisdom

The Bible says of Mary, the mother of Jesus, that she "treasured up all these things and pondered them in her heart" (Luke 2:19). *Ponder* means to consider, think about, muse, deliberate, and wonder. So today, this week, consider, muse, and ponder your guy and appreciate the way God wired him. Then tell him. Anytime something precious comes to mind about him, voice it.

Wow Date

Create a date that celebrates the word you have selected to describe your husband's essence:

- If *courageous*—plan something daring.
- If *compassionate*—treat him to a mission of mercy.
- If *creative*—plan a trip to the art museum, symphony, or other favorite place where creative juices flow.

I never really understood why years ago Bill and I found an afternoon in the seminary library romantic. Now I know: Wisdom and God's love met there. I am going on a Google hunt now. I may need to use MapQuest to find that special place where the longitude of wisdom meets the latitude of love. When I locate it, I'm taking my loving, wise Bill there.

Where are you going?

Wow 27

Foreplay

Couples have lost the art of foreplay. In an instant gratification world we rush everything, even lovemaking. Foreplay is that precious warm up to intercourse, but I think it is much more than this. Foreplay is what keeps a marriage hot, sizzling hot, red-hot, year after year.

Sexual intercourse, as we all know, can be pulled off in a few basic positions. We may have heard of or read the *Kama Sutra* or gotten a book that claims 52 or even 365 new ways to have sex, but most of those would require you to be contortionists. It is foreplay that makes lovemaking an art, along with all the interesting nuances and interactions.

Wow Assignment

This week, choose to go without sex for a few days. ("Pam," you say, "that's normal for us.") OK, but this time add in the flirt, the compliments, the passing hand on his shoulder, the swish across his backside, the rubbing of his shoulders or feet. Nibble his neck, whisper in his ear, caress his inner thigh. Tickle him (if he enjoys that), or walk arm-in-arm or with your arm around his waist. Hold and caress his hand. Run your fingernail up his arm, down his back, or up his zipper. Put some planning into this. Think of as many ways as you can to touch, caress, and fondle him in a "Baby, I want you" kind of way.

Wow Wisdom

This really isn't my idea. In Song of Solomon, we see the couple, King Solomon and his wife, Shulamite, enjoying all kinds of foreplay:

> Let him kiss me with the kisses of his mouth—
> for your love is more delightful than wine.
> (1:2)

> Strengthen me with raisins,
> refresh me with apples,
> for I am faint with love.
> His left arm is under my head,
> and his right arm embraces me.
> (2:5-6)

> I said, "I will climb the palm tree;
> I will take hold of its fruit."
> May your breasts be like clusters of grapes on the vine,
> the fragrance of your breath like apples,
> and your mouth like the best wine.
> (7:8-9)

> Come, my beloved, let us go to the countryside,
> let us spend the night in the villages.
> (7:11)

Wow Date

Invite your guy on a date without saying a word. Try using just your touch to wow him and lure him into the bedroom.

Love Under Pressure

While I was writing this book, Bill noticed that I was going to be just shy of the necessary 100,000 annual travel miles to keep my Executive Platinum frequent flier status with American Airlines. Being Executive Platinum means we usually get upgraded to first class, but most importantly, if something goes wrong while traveling, we are first in line to get the solution to our dilemma. Last year, we were away from home for ministry over two hundred days, so we need all the help we can get to ensure we are where we're supposed to be when we're supposed to be there.

Our anniversary is in December, so Bill planned a five-day, five-city, back and forth from coast to coast trip logging over 12,000 miles. I dubbed the trip, "Love is in the air."

Wow Assignment

For most people, schlepping your suitcases in and out of airline terminals, riding mass transit, renting cars, and napping in airport lounges at odd hours is not their version of romance. But let me share what I was reminded of on this trip:

Bill is *ingenious*. To plan a trip where we never were in one place more than twenty-four hours guaranteed no jet lag.

Bill is *thrifty*. He scheduled flights so that most meals were the ones served in first class, saving us money so the meals we did enjoy in each city were romantic, top of the line.

Bill is a *problem solver*. When our bags were lost on the second to last leg, his positive, "glass is half-full" attitude created the idea of soaking in the Jacuzzi tub while our clothes were in the washer and dryer. Soaking me and my clothes simultaneously was a great use of time. Let's just say I didn't care that my bag was missing!

Bill is a *servant*. He had logged plenty of miles speaking for Promise Keepers in Canada, but he set aside his desire for a longer trip to Europe or Hawaii (or here at home in sunny California) for one that would serve my needs and get me across the Executive Platinum finish line.

Under pressure, what are your mate's best qualities?

Wow Wisdom

Pressure does bring to the surface a person's strongest qualities. Here's why: "Consider it pure joy, my brothers and sisters, whenever you face trials of many kinds, because you know that the testing of your faith produces perseverance. Let perseverance finish its work so that you may be mature and complete, not lacking anything" (James 1:2-4).

Pressure produces maturity.

Wow Date

Plan a date that puts your love under pressure. Do something romantic that requires a schedule or itinerary or do something romantic that pushes you both physically, such as backpacking, biking, or hiking. Perhaps a date to create something lasting would do it: add on a room, tackle that painting project together, work on the cars. The task is not what's important. What's vital is to compliment all along the path the core strength, the stamina, the inner determination you see in your man.

Wow 29

Happy Holidays

Carlie "surprises" Nick with a trip each birthday to a place he can golf and they can make love in someplace warmer than their snowy hometown. Mandy and Josh make love under the lights of the Christmas tree each Christmas Eve—which meant later and later rendezvous as the kids got older, then finally a private tree in their bedroom.

Amy runs a bubble bath for her man every New Year's Eve, and then they make love at the stroke of midnight, ringing in the New Year with their own fireworks. Erica and Leo make love under the stars every Independence Day, sometimes timing their personal pyrotechnics to those blazing across the summer sky.

Carol and Jim stay in a five-star hotel every February 13 so they wake up to romance on Valentine's Day. The O'Malleys have their own version of "find the lucky shamrock" on Saint Patrick's Day, as they hide shamrock stickers on their bodies and invite their mate to locate them in hopes of "getting lucky."

After tucking in the kids on October 31, Claire and Pat raid the candy dish and eat dessert as they nibble on their lover's favorite sweet spots. Even happily married Jenn and Henry admit one of the secrets to the success of their fifty-year marriage is their Sunday afternoon "nap."

Wow Assignment

How can you make yearly holidays nights to remember? By weaving in some simple traditions—especially red-hot romantic ones—that become secret encounters only the two of you know about and look forward to.

- Dress up (then undress) for the Emmys or Academy Awards—even if you'll never be a Hollywood star. Listen to the Country Music Awards in the back of a pickup on some country road and act out the lyrics of the most romantic "roll in the hay" tunes.

- Buy season tickets to the symphony, summer pops, or a jazz series or for your favorite sports team. Take in the Final Four, the Triple Crown, or a NASCAR race. And be sure to book a night's stay in a nearby hotel.

- Or create your own tradition to a lesser-known holiday like:

  - National Do Nothing Day
  - National Give a Hug Day
  - Kiss Your Mate Day
  - Date Your Mate Month (It's May, by the way.)

Wow Wisdom

Psalm 77:11 says, "I will *remember* the deeds of the LORD." God thinks it's wise to commemorate. In the Old Testament, there are numerous festivals and holidays. Purim, for example, marks the date Israel was saved from extinction, an event we read about in the book of Esther. What do you want to remember?

Wow Date

What is your husband's favorite holiday? How can you make it even more memorable? Or Google unusual or bizarre holidays and see if you can create a new fun tradition year after year.

Wow 30

Blue Moon

Songs have been written about the celestial body of romance: "Blue Moon," "Moon River," "Paper Moon," "Dancing in the Moonlight," "Moonlight and Roses," "By the Light of the Silvery Moon"...the list goes on and on.

Why not move the moon into your romantic rhythm? Here are some moonlit nights to remember:

- Full moon (It takes twenty-nine days, twelve hours, and forty-four minutes between full moons, which creates the concept of a month.)

- Crescent moon

- Harvest moon

- Blue moon (This happens every two to three years as the extra minutes accumulate to add a second full moon in a calendar month.)

- Lunar eclipse (This happens between four and seven times a year.)

Wow Assignment

See if you can come up with a creative way to celebrate your man each moon. *National Geographic* lists some historical names for each month's special moon:

January: Wolf Moon—Named after the howling of hungry wolves lamenting the lack of food. Other names: old moon and ice moon.

February: Snow Moon—The typically cold, snowy weather earned the name snow moon. Other names: storm moon and hunger moon.

March: Worm Moon—The last full moon of winter was named after the worm trails in the newly thawed ground. Other names: death moon, crust moon (a reference to crusty snow), and sap moon (after the tapping of the maple trees).

April: Pink Moon—Named for blooming wildflower. Other names: sprouting-grass moon, the egg moon, and fish moon.

May: Flower Moon—Abundant blooms give this month's full moon its name. Other names include the hare moon, the corn-planting moon, and the milk moon.

June: Strawberry Moon—The harvesting of strawberries gives this name. Other names: rose moon or hot moon for the beginning of the summer heat.

July: Buck Moon—Male deer regrow antlers in July. Other names include thunder moon and hay moon, after the July hay harvest.

August: Sturgeon Moon—North American fishing tribes named this moon for the abundance of fish. Other names: green-corn moon, grain moon, red moon (the hue it often takes on in the summer haze).

September: Harvest Moon—The familiar name for when crops are gathered. It also refers to the moon's bright appearance and early rise, which lets farmers continue harvesting into evening. Other names include the corn moon and the barley moon.

October: Hunter's Moon—The preferred month to hunt with the help of the bright night sky. Other names include the travel moon and the dying-grass moon.

November: Beaver Moon—Native Americans set beaver traps during this month. Another name is the frost moon.

December: Cold Moon—The coming of winter earned this moniker. Other names include the long-night moon and the oak moon.[25]

Wow Wisdom

Numbers 10:10 refers to the people of God celebrating in connection with lunar markings: "Also at your times of rejoicing—your appointed festivals and New Moon feasts—you are to sound the trumpets over your burnt offerings and fellowship offerings, and they will be a memorial for you before your God. I am the LORD your God."

Wow Date

Plan a date that celebrates the moon that might have been up the night you met, first kissed, or married. Or look up the lunar charts and see if a full moon can be celebrated with your honey this week. If privacy is still possible, open the curtains, lift the shades, and make love by the light of the silvery moon.

Wow 31

Make It Good

Women's Health published the results of a commonsense study that revealed that women who greeted their spouse "good morning" as they started their day had better days than those who didn't. Of those couples who say good morning to each other, 94 percent rate their relationship as excellent.[26] A positive greeting sets an upbeat tone for the entire day.

My friend Karen Porter has that perky sunrise attitude:

> George and I married forty-four years ago after a whirlwind engagement. I asked George to think of all the things that had happened in those forty-four years and tell me which one had wowed him. His answer: "Karen, the thing that pleases me most is that you wake up every day happy and cheerful and full of joy. It makes every day a day of wow." Years ago I decided to stop being cranky and not to make him miserable. I chose joy instead. So every morning, I choose to wake up with a bright-eyed anticipation. In my book, *I'll Bring the Chocolate*, I wrote, "Joyful living becomes a conscious decision; it means choosing joy...

even when we may not feel like it." The Bible says, "Rejoice, and again I say rejoice."

Wow Assignment

How many ways can you think of to wow your man in the morning?

- Wake him with a kiss and a smile.
- Wake him slowly with some foreplay.
- Bring him coffee in bed.
- Bring him breakfast in bed.
- Write a note in the steam on the mirror as he showers.
- Shower with him.
- Give a morning massage.
- Help him get out the door by assisting him in finding what he needs.
- Send a text greeting him—or waking him with that familiar "bing."
- Work out with him.
- Go on a morning prayer walk.

Wow Wisdom

My sister-in-law Erin is a great role model for wives. My brother Bret had a heart attack at forty, mostly due to our family's horrible DNA, but some due to the rising responsibility of his professional life and lowered activity rate. Once he was out of the hospital, Erin began getting up at 5:00 a.m. each day to walk four miles with him. They walk and pray for each other. They have always had a strong marriage, but there is a spark and a sizzle in their love that few experience at midlife and beyond. It can be seen in their smiles, their glances, the way they pass and touch. Their love is truly inspiring, and I believe one secret is the way they begin their day.

This should be no surprise as God greets us each morning with hope. The book of Lamentations proclaims that God's "compassions never fail. They are new every morning" (Lamentations 3:22-23). We reflect God's love when we give compassion each morning to the man we love.

Wow Date

Have an early morning date. Find a morning that isn't quite as rushed and do something special. Tailor the morning to his desires, so if he is a late riser, serve him breakfast in bed followed by a little red-hot monogamy. If he is an early bird, get up and enjoy a sunrise with him, work out, shower, then do a "bedroom workout" and shower again! Plan ahead. The night before, place on your nightstand mints, a towel, massage oil, or whatever you might need, then pray for him as you drift to sleep so your heart is ready to wow him in the morning.

Wow 32

That's Puzzling

Wikipedia suggests that "a *puzzle* is a problem or enigma that tests the ingenuity of the solver. In a basic puzzle, one is intended to put together pieces in a logical way in order to come up with the desired solution."[27] Yep, your man is a puzzle. And puzzles can be either entertaining—or a disciplined, focused search for a logical solution or answer to a perplexing quandary.

The word *puzzle* dates back to the sixteenth century,[28] but we all know the reality of life being a puzzle goes back to Eden. Adam couldn't figure out how to lead his woman, and Eve couldn't figure out why she should listen to her man (or her God for that matter). Life and love can be confusing, so instead of fighting it, celebrate that your mate and your love is a beautiful puzzle of hearts.

Wow Assignment

Think of the various kinds of puzzles:

- Stick or construction puzzles like the popular game Jenga or pick-up sticks
- Jigsaw puzzles
- 3-D puzzles like the Rubik's Cube

- Logic puzzles like chess or checkers
- Paper-and-pencil puzzles like the simple connect the dots, hangman, or tic-tac-toe
- Word puzzles and crossword puzzles
- Card games like solitaire

Wow Wisdom

Paul says in Colossians 1:27, "To them God has chosen to make known among the Gentiles the glorious riches of this mystery, which is Christ in you, the hope of glory." Christ living in us was a mystery until God revealed it to us. In the same way, husbands are a mystery until God tells us how to love them, and God has told us that what husbands need most is respect. In Ephesians 5:33, Paul simply says "the wife must respect her husband."

In our book *The Marriage Code*, Bill and I explain that the code that unlocks a man's heart, life, and mind is success. If we wives meet that success need first, our man will be easier to live with, easier to love. If we respect our man enough to help him succeed in life, in career, in the community, in the family, and with us, it helps set him up to succeed in the calling God has given him as a husband: to love his wife as Christ loved the church.

For ages women have been puzzled by the concept of submission or respecting their man, but if we do it, we gain God's supernatural perspective on our man so he is not so enigmatic. The puzzle will be solved, and we will find that love we desperately seek.

Wow Date

Take some puzzle pieces, such as Jenga logs or jigsaw pieces, and write a message to your man inviting him out for an evening of puzzlement. Use the night to thank him, praise him, or lead him to a romantic setting via puzzles that celebrate your love together. Maybe play a puzzle game with him where the winner gets sex his or her way. (Hint: Ensure your man wins!)

Leave Him Alone

Yes, this might sound counterintuitive to a relationship book, but honestly, sometimes what your man wants is to be left alone. Let him sleep in, give him that nap, let him snooze in his recliner or the hammock. Ignore the mess he is making in the shed, the garage, or the barn. Bite your tongue as he plays hours of Xbox, online gaming, or Fantasy Football. That's right, let him be a little boy. Let him play mindlessly if he wants, for hours or even an entire day (yes, it will be difficult to endure, but go with me on this). Let your significant interaction be to give him a kiss as you hand him a beverage or slide a plate of food in front of him.

Wow Assignment

For a week, keep track of what your man chooses to do when he has a couple spare minutes. For a while, I noticed Bill would pull up a solitaire game on his phone or computer screen when he felt stuck in the task at hand or had writer's block. If I would walk in, he would switch to a "more productive" task.

One day I asked him in a nonaccusatory, nonjudgmental way, "Honey, tell me about that game. What is it? Why do you enjoy it?"

He explained how it helped him clear his mind, and it actually helped lower his blood pressure (we know this because at the time his doctor had him taking readings several times a day).

Well, any game that will help my man think better and keep him alive longer is not a waste of time or a frivolous pursuit—it is a smart choice for a few minutes of relaxation.

Wow Wisdom

God calls each of us aside for times of rest and renewal. David penned a well-known poem about it when he proclaimed,

> He makes me lie down in green pastures,
>> he leads me beside quiet waters,
>> he refreshes my soul.
>
> (Psalm 23:2-3)

Notice the verb, God "makes" David lie down. It is imperative to give the freedom to your guy to schedule in some well-deserved downtime.

Wow Date

You might be familiar with the yoga pose called *shavasana,* which is simply to lie down, close your eyes, and purposefully relax every muscle in your body. Here's a news flash: Eastern religion didn't create this activity. God did! So take back what is God's and rest with your guy. Climb into a hammock and gaze at the clouds. Fall back in the grass and soak in the sun. Lean on the rocks or beach wall and take in a sunset. Flop onto the bed, take a breather, and snuggle up in his arms, offering to scratch his chest or back or give a back or foot massage.

Rest, relax, and renew your guy.

Wow 34

Oh How Tweet!

ere's some interesting information about the use of Twitter, a popular social-networking tool, in the workplace today:

- 57 percent of workers who use Twitter spend at least forty minutes a week on the site.
- 300,000 new users sign up for Twitter each day.
- 5 percent of Americans knew what Twitter was in 2008 compared to 87 percent in 2010.
- More than half of Twitter users are under age forty-five.
- Twitter's search engine processes 600 million queries a day.
- 37 percent of Twitter users tweet from their phones.[29]

To tweet is to post up to 140 characters on the Twitter.com website. Those who "follow" you receive this post on their smartphone or computer. One might wonder if anything helpful can come in 140 characters, but here is some advice I have posted on relationships on my Twitter account @PamFarrel:[30]

- "I will show you my faith by my deeds" (James 2:18). In the same way, your actions will speak louder than your words to your man.

- We marry the person of our dreams, then grow discontent because we forget the dream in light of reality.

- Prayer is like a window to the heart of your spouse.

- "Walking out doesn't help; wherever you go, you take yourself with you" (*The 10 Best Decisions a Couple Can Make*).

- "Forgiveness protects your integrity and your heart" (*The 10 Best Decisions a Couple Can Make*).

- "Forgiveness frees you to go forward in life and in all relationships" (*Love, Honor and Forgive*).

- "I began praying for hubby instead of trying to be the Holy Spirit" (*The 10 Best Decisions a Couple Can Make*).

- The strongest marriages = 2 people who love being 2gether.

- Remember, no husband's ever been shot while doing dishes. LOL

- "Don't look at problems, look at the potential of your love" (*The 10 Best Decisions a Couple Can Make*).

- Romance = seeing the masterpiece God's given u in ur spouse & taking time to applaud it.

- A secret to long-lasting love is to enjoy the daily delights of your love.

Wow Assignment

If you have a Twitter account (or even if you don't), what would you tweet about your man? Here are a few ideas:

- @BFarrel: GR8 honor being married to a gr8 man.

- My hubby @BFarrel can fix anything: the car, the house, the furnace, the sprinklers, the driveway—and people's hearts and lives.

Wow Wisdom

God has His own version of Twitter: Proverbs! These couplets offer powerful advice such as:

> Gracious words are a honeycomb,
>> sweet to the soul and healing to the bones.
>>> (Proverbs 16:24)

So use your words, few as they might be, wisely.

Wow Date

What would you tweet to your husband that would make him smile? (Yes, *please* direct tweet so it is private! If you are unsure how to direct tweet, you can also text these phone-to-phone to ensure privacy.)

- Meet me. Our place, your style, now.
- U R 1 GR8 Guy. 4get work. Meet me @ home @ 5. Clothing optional.
- Got ur fav meal ready. Dessert is on me—literally.
- Hey hottie! Come fan my flame. Let's get sparks flying.
- How can 1 woman be so 4tunate? U R gr8 guy w gr8 heart, gr8 mind & gr8 bod!

Plan his favorite meal or activity and tweet or text the invite home. It will B GR8!

Wow 35

Own It!

It's easy for us women to see the areas our husband needs to improve. We are quick to point out *his* flaws, *his* shortcomings, *his* mistakes, and we often give ourselves a pass on areas that are frustrating our husband. It might be because we know change is hard. We put off our need to change until the pain to change is less severe than the pain of staying in the status quo.

Wow Assignment

For years, I wanted Bill to make more money so we weren't so stressed as a new little family with preschoolers. I wanted him to change, not me. We had decided we wanted to be with our children as much as possible, so we made the decision together to have me be an at-home mom when the kids were small. For the most part, I was frugal in expenditures, and I prided myself in finding a sale or a deal before I bought anything. But I had a fatal flaw. I would often forget to write down when I wrote a check or how much the check was for. I excused myself by explaining my hands were full with toddlers and a baby—I just didn't have time to record such details! But this flimsy excuse didn't help Bill at all when it came time to pay the bills or reconcile the checkbook.

Wow Wisdom

After a few years of on and off frustration for Bill, I prayed:

> Search me, God, and know my heart;
> test me and know my anxious thoughts.
> See if there is any offensive way in me,
> and lead me in the way everlasting.
> (Psalm 139:23-24)

I asked God to give me some ideas on better ways to handle money so Bill wouldn't be surprised by my shopping. After praying, I approached Bill with some ideas:

- Create cash envelopes for things I typically spent money on: groceries, gifts, clothes. When the cash was gone, shopping was done!
- Get duplicate checks so if I forgot to record in the checkbook registry there was a carbon copy of who I wrote the check to and the amount and the date I wrote it.

These were simple to implement. They were reachable, attainable goals. (I did have to learn to slide the plastic divider underneath each check so the duplicate was legible.) Change in me produced a positive change in Bill.

Wow Date

What small change is God asking you to make that might make a big difference in the overall atmosphere of your relationship? Invite your man out to celebrate the change (it can't be just a promise; you have to have made some headway on the change first). To celebrate the change in how I managed our checking account, I voided a check and turned it into an invitation to use a two-for-one dinner coupon.

My neighbor Debbie also made a big change in a big way:

> I was not always supportive of what I saw as my husband's

crazy passions...When our [children] were in their teens, I no longer felt that I loved my husband. I was desperately unhappy and had nowhere else to turn for help but the Lord. That verse in 1 Peter jumped out at me: "Wives respect your husbands." I had nothing to lose. I didn't have to love him, but I could choose to respect him...I not only began to respect my husband in situations that I normally saw only weakness, but slowly but surely I also began to have *love* for my husband in a way that I never had before. My husband blossomed before my very eyes.

Years later, this change of heart created a change of course: Mike had always dreamt of one day selling real estate. He had gotten his license when the kids were little, but it never seemed like the right time to jump ship, what with private school tuition and mortgage payments. Years and years passed, and he thought perhaps it would stay a dream. Our home burned down in the San Diego fires of 2003, and with the kids grown and on their own by then, we decided why not start over—all over? Many thought we were nuts, but we both quit our secure jobs and jumped into real estate while we rebuilt our home. We felt a bit like newlyweds!

Create a date that helps your husband see and enjoy the change in you.

Take a Break from
Facebook...and Face Him

Facebook is a powerful and growing phenomenon. Every sixty seconds, Facebook has 510,404 comments posted, 382,861 are "liked," 135,849 photos are uploaded, 98,604 friendships are approved, 82,557 status updates are made, 79,364 wall posts are created, 74,204 invitations are sent. As of December 2010, one out of every dozen people had a Facebook account. Every day 700,000 new people sign up—and they speak seventy-five different languages.

"If Facebook were a country, it would be the third largest,"[31] asserts *Time* magazine. *Time* also estimates that Facebook will gain its one billionth member in 2012—and the world has roughly six billion people! Facebook is a force, a power, and as the wise uncle in Spiderman says, "with great power comes great responsibility."

Wow Assignment

With the growth of Facebook has come the growth of Facebook dysfunction:

Relationships on Facebook have a seductive, addictive

quality that can erode or even replace real world relationships...An article published earlier this year in *European Psychiatry* presented the case of a woman who lost her job to a Facebook addiction, and the authors suggested that it could become an actual diagnosable ailment. (The woman in question couldn't even make it through an examination without checking her Facebook on her phone.)[32]

This addictive behavior is further evidenced by a study that showed one-third of all women checked Facebook even before they went to the bathroom in the morning when they woke up![33]

Facebook has also had a significant negative impact on marriages: "According to the American Academy of Matrimonial Lawyers, 81% of its members have seen a rise in the number of divorce cases involving social networking; 66% cite Facebook as the primary source for online divorce evidence."[34]

Another study notes a rise in narcissism with the rise of Facebook use[35]—or could it be Facebook just provides the perfect platform for a narcissist?

Wow Wisdom

Don't blame Facebook founder Mark Zuckerberg for these relationship maladies. His vision is actually pretty well balanced and altruistic:

> What we are trying to do is map out all those trust relationships...The thing I really care about is making the world more open and connected...open means having access to more information...connected is helping people stay in touch and maintain empathy...Having two identities for yourself is an example of a lack of integrity.[36]

Mark seems to have a heart that is in the right place: be yourself, your authentic self, on and off the net; have empathy; and apply the Golden Rule, which might be paraphrased, "Post unto others as you would have others post unto you."

Wow Date

Go on a Facebook fast for one week. (You can do it!) In real time, interface with your mate Facebook style:

- *Update your status:* Tell your mate just how much you love being connected to him.

- *Comment:* Reflect and positively reply to your man.

- *Chat:* Take him out for talk time in his favorite location.

- *Upload a picture:* Go on a date that is "Facebook worthy" from your husband's point of view. Enjoy taking pictures of real life and real fun. This time, instead of posting to Facebook, print and talk about your memories and why you loved what you loved with *just* your man as the audience.

- *Link:* Have a heart-to-heart, hand-to-hand, body-to-body interaction (and don't tell *anyone*!).

Wow 37

Treasure Hunt

My friend Jody planned a special date for her husband:

I had written a poem or riddle to send him on a treasure hunt of memories we had shared in the past. I went to his work and handed him a note with instructions to change into the shirt that was waiting for him in the car.

Once he got to the car and changed, there was another love note that took him to the country club where we met and had our first date. We shared a glass of wine and a dance. I left him with a note for instructions to his next destination, and then I dashed out the door to light candles at his next stop, which was at the lake where we had shared many romantic dates in the past.

When he arrived at the lake there was another love-note poem to take him to his next destination...the church where we exchanged our wedding vows...I placed it on the foyer table with a statue of a bride and groom, our wedding picture, and his next love note. (This was comical, because I didn't know they had Bible study in the sanctuary where he was searching for his next clue, and everyone in the Bible study stopped to help him look.)

That love note brought him back home to a candlelight dinner, passionate lovemaking, and one last note (in poem form).

Wow Assignment

What is a treasure to your man? Where would he like the clues to lead? Would he love to be in a race car? On a football field? On a wave? At a car show? In a home improvement store?

In the military, the action first happens in the war room. What would be his "wow war room"?

Wow Wisdom

Jody was motivated because she took time to reflect. Here is how she worded her inspiration:

> Why did I do this, you might ask? Because this man has loved me like my heart has always hungered for…just loving me for who God created me to be, without changing me. He wakes up every day with joy in his heart, comes home from a job he isn't crazy about, and still dances with me in the kitchen to no music with the kids in the room, so they can see what it is like for a husband and wife to express love to each other, all because God calls him to be the husband and father that is willing to sacrifice and to love unconditionally. I am blessed![37]

Reflect on what would make you spend hours to wow your man and lead him to his treasure by writing down why he is a treasure to you.

Wow Date

To design a treasure hunt, you can plot and plan it many ways:

- Clues can be in the form of a riddle.
- Clues can be hints planted with people ahead of time.
- Clues can be hidden around town and lead from one to another.
- Clues can be given in text messages.
- Clues can be given "kidnapper style" by directing him to show up at a payphone and wait for a call.

This week get a clue and give your man his treasure.

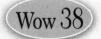

Wow 38

Ride Down
Memory Lane

Julie and Mike had been married for twenty-four years when she sent me the email describing her most creative wow date for her guy:

> When I met my husband, he was a "wild at heart" twenty-four-year old whose primary source of transportation was a very fast motorcycle! Shortly after children arrived on the scene, we sold the bike and bought a used mini-truck, which was much more suited to carrying bicycles, golden retrievers, and other "kid stuff." It must have been hard for him, but he never complained. Our most creative date came just after we sent our youngest child off to kindergarten.
>
> On the morning of our anniversary I gave him a card with money I had secretly saved up and directions to our first destination—a motorcycle shop where I had arranged to rent a Harley-Davidson for the weekend. It was such a thrill to see the smile on his face as we climbed onto that bike. It took us back to the time when we fell in love! Our final stop was a little romantic cabin in the mountains where we

celebrated—kid, dog, and truck free! I was blessed to be able to remind him that I will never forget who he *is* or the many selfless sacrifices he makes for our family.[38]

Wow Assignment

What does your man need to remember about himself? Take him back...back to:

- The stadium
- The ranch
- The racetrack
- The road
- The wilderness
- The mountains
- The ocean or lake

Wow Wisdom

Jesus used this "take them back" technique with Peter to prepare him for the future He had planned for him—leadership in the early church. It started with Jesus asking His followers, His disciples,

"Who do people say the Son of Man is?"

They replied, "Some say John the Baptist; others say Elijah; and still others, Jeremiah or one of the prophets."

"But what about you?" he asked. "Who do you say I am?"

Simon Peter answered, "You are the Messiah, the Son of the living God."

Jesus replied, "Blessed are you, Simon son of Jonah, for this was not revealed to you by flesh and blood, but by my Father in heaven. And I tell you that you are Peter, and on this rock I will build my church, and the gates of Hades will not overcome it."

(Matthew 16:13-18)

Peter's name means "rock." What does your man's name mean? Peter needed to remember he was a rock. What does your guy need to remember?

Wow Date

Take him back to where he loved to be when you first met him and let him enjoy some of his first loves. Tell him what you first saw in him. You might also compliment him on how he has become what his parents named him.

I first laid eyes on Bill at a leadership conference at Arrowhead Springs. He was there to learn how to be a Christian leader—and his name, William, means "guardian of the gospel." It was a romantic day and meaningful date to rewalk the grounds at Arrowhead, this time as a pastor and his wife.

Wow 39

R-E-S-P-E-C-T!

Aretha Franklin sang it. Otis Redding wrote it. We women have a hard time giving it: R-E-S-P-E-C-T. Women often hear, "You need to respect your husband," but I have discovered that is not an easy task for most women, including me. Here is a story adapted from our book *Men Are Like Waffles—Women Are Like Spaghetti* that shares how God clued me in to just how to respect my man. First you'll hear Bill's side:

> When Pam and I moved to the San Diego area so I could begin my career as a senior pastor, I was very excited. She was the primary caretaker of our two preschool boys, and we were living in a two-bedroom apartment with a very awkward "rule." The "rule" was that children were not allowed to play on the sidewalk, on the grass, or in the common areas of the apartment complex. Now, Pam is usually a very positive individual, but the stress of dealing with two toddlers in a "no playing zone" (and no car) was more than she could handle. A depression blindsided her. Instead of her being proud of me, I heard things like, "Why did you do this to me?" "How long do we have to live like this?"

Wow Assignment

I (Pam) had given up a nice house, great friends, and a satisfying leadership role for sanctified insanity! Over the next few weeks, a depression hit me like a tidal wave. One day I went to the closet to get something off the top shelf. The next thing I knew, I was sitting on a load of dirty laundry and I was sobbing! I don't know how long I sat there, but in toddled my two little boys.

"Mommy, what's wrong?" they asked.

I moaned, "I don't know."

I gathered them onto my lap, and I rocked them and prayed. *God, I know this is not the abundant life You planned. Bill has been paying a huge price. He's been coming home to complaints and my whining. I have believed lies about him. I've said some awful things, like "You don't care about me!" (and I know he does) and "Your job is more important than me and the kids!" (that is definitely not true).* I looked around my pathetic setting and cried out to God, *Help me figure out what to do!*

I sat and rocked my boys to sleep, then put them to bed. I pulled out my Bible and read a familiar passage in Ephesians 5. One phrase seemed to be in neon lights: "the wife must respect her husband." I looked at it again. *Are you sure about this, God? Isn't there a loophole for situations like mine?*

Over the next few days, I consulted a dictionary and a thesaurus, looking up synonyms of *respect*. I came up with three things I needed to do:

- *See Bill as God sees Bill*—a man worthy of honor because God created him.

- *Speak to Bill the way God talks to Bill*—with loving, encouraging, but honest words.

- *Serve Bill as God treats Bill*—by building him up with kindness.

Which area of respect do you need to work on?

Wow Wisdom

A few days later, I thought of a way to apply Ephesians 5 and honor my man: I called Bill up and asked to take him to lunch. Over lunch, I reached across the table, took his hand, and said, "I'm sorry for the way I have treated you. I just want you to know, if I never get the things I think will make me happy, that's okay. From this day forward I am on *your* team!"

Wow Date

How can you show your man you are on *his* team? Here are some ideas of things you can do:

- *See him as God sees him.* Make a date at a place with a great view!
- *Speak to him as God would.* Add in a letter or poem to build him up, and read it aloud.
- *Serve him as God would.* Take him to a place symbolic of what is most valuable to him.

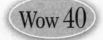

Light His Fire

Songs are written about it—"Come on Baby, Light My Fire!" "Fire," Elvis's "Hunka Burning Love." Love has been compared to it—"My love is a consuming fire" or "I am burning with desire" are familiar expressions of endearment. Romance includes it—lovemaking by the fire, dinner by candlelight, or a bedroom lit with candles.

Wow Assignment

We encourage you to fan the flame of love and stoke the fire of your burning desire by creating a red-hot code word that indicates you are interested in some sizzling sex.

In our book *Red-Hot Monogamy,* we give examples of code words that clue your mate to the internal combustion going on in your body. Our favorite code word comes from our book *Men Are Like Waffles— Women Are Like Spaghetti* where we explain how men and women relieve stress differently. Women talk their way through stress, but men like to go to their easy boxes to recharge: the TV, the computer, the garage, the football field, the refrigerator, and the bed. That bed box for sex is like the free square of a bingo card, and men can get to it from every square on their waffle.

While sharing this at one seminar, anytime we'd come close to the topic of sex, the audience would shout, "Bingo!" One couple bought us a plaque that read "Born to Bingo." And when we spoke on a cruise liner, another couple bought shirts off the recreation staff to give to us that read, "Have you been bingoed today?" So our code phrase is, "Want to play some bingo?" We can simply slide a bingo card under the office door and the work day is over!

Once when we were teaching this in the south, the church we were in played a form of *The Dating Game*. The women were asked, "What is your husband's perfect date?" One by one the women answered: "We'd go to dinner, but I think we might come home early," or "I think we might do a movie, but we'd come home early." The last husband that answered said, "Well, dinner and movie, but we'd come home early and light a fire in the fireplace and a fire on the couch!" I told the audience, "I learned a bit about southerners today. Ya'll don't have sex, you just 'come home early' and 'light fires'!"

Any form of a flame might work for you too. One couple we know collects candles from each place they travel, and when one is in the mood, she or he simply starts lighting those candles located throughout their home.

Wow Wisdom

The concept of a code word for sex isn't ours. Solomon and his bride use it in Song of Solomon 6:2:

> My beloved has gone down to his garden,
> to the beds of spices,
> to browse in the gardens
> and to gather lilies.

Any gardening term could be used as an invitation to enjoy each other's "gardens," the sexual areas of each other's bodies. (Perhaps wow him by *coming home early* to a *fire* in the *garden* and play *bingo!*)

Wow Date

Ignite your passion with some red-hot clues and have a smokin' hot date by a fireplace, by candlelight, or by a bonfire or campfire with a sleeping bag for two.

Wow 41

Get a Plan for Love

One of the complaints we sometimes hear from husbands is their wives are either so type A that *everything* is an A priority and life is too intense or their wife seems fickle and flighty and doesn't get much accomplished. To find a balance that will work for both of you, you might want to create a date to jot down your answers to the goal-setting questions on the worksheet below. We have used this over our thirty-one years together, and it helps us get and stay on the same page. You two can become a couple that works well as a team to accomplish God's purpose and plan.

Wow Assignment

Complete this worksheet:

1. As you look at the year ahead, what is the most important issue or goal you have on your heart for *yourself*?

    Wife:

    Husband:

2. As you look at the year ahead, what is the most important issue or goal you have on your heart for *our marriage*?

    Wife:

    Husband:

3. As you look at the year ahead, what is the most important issue or goal you have on your heart for *our family*?

    Wife:

    Husband:

4. What adjustments on the home front would make reaching these desires easier?

    Wife:

    Husband:

5. How are you planning to grow yourself:

    Spiritually?
    Wife:

    Husband:

    Physically?
    Wife:

    Husband:

    Emotionally?
    Wife:

    Husband:

Socially?
Wife:

Husband:

Academically or in your career?
Wife:

Husband:

6. What can I do to help you?
Wife:

Husband:

On a separate sheet, write these desires into tangible, measurable goals.

Create a personal, family, or marriage *motto* for the year. Here are some examples: *Family Is First and Fine in 2009* (for a busy couple); *Marriage and Money Are Great in '08* (for a couple wanting to get out of debt). A married couple who was drifting apart made theirs, *Love Again in 2010*—and guess what? They went from the brink of divorce to a vibrant and loving marriage before the Thanksgiving holiday.

Your motto:

Do you have a verse for the year that captures what you think God is saying to your heart? Place a few key words into the word search on www .Biblegateway.com, and you'll get a list of verses to select from. Here's one of ours from a year we needed to take better care of ourselves: "Beloved,

I pray that in all respects you may prosper and be in good health, just as your soul prospers" (3 John 2 NASB).

Your verse:

Then memorize the verse and meditate on it daily.

Wow Wisdom

A single word can empower your love. Choose a word that sums up your mutual goal for the year, such as *integrity*, *authenticity*, or *family*.

Your word is:

Wow Date

Set aside a date to complete the goal-setting worksheet. Add to the fun by including a way to succeed at these new goals. Use the word you selected above as your password, or create a screen saver or mouse pad with your motto on it. Find or create a wall hanging with your verse on it. Record yourself saying your goals, motto, verse, or word onto your computer or smartphone. Celebrate all your hard work of goal setting with the purchase of a new calendar and write in fun dates to look forward to all year.

If your hubby isn't all that excited about goal setting, make it worth his while by asking him what he would like to be rewarded with for the time investment in both setting and accomplishing the goals. We are all motivated by rewards. It's time to find out what reward will wow your guy.

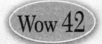

Wow 42

Laugh a Little

A country preacher decided to skip services one Sunday and head to the hills to do some bear hunting. As he rounded the corner on a perilous twist in the trail, he and a bear collided, sending him and his rifle tumbling down the mountainside. His rifle went one way and he went the other, and when he looked up, the ferocious bear was charging at him.

"O Lord," the preacher prayed, "I'm so sorry for skipping services today to come out here and hunt. Please forgive me and grant me just one wish...please make a Christian out of that bear. Please, Lord!"

Just then the bear skidded to a halt, fell to its knees, clasped its paws together, and began to pray aloud right at the preacher's feet, "Dear Lord, bless this food I am about to receive. In Jesus' name, amen."

OK, that's funny! Come on, you at least smiled, right? Humor is good for our bodies—and for our relationships. Dr. Paul McGhee says, "Your sense of humor is one of the most powerful tools you have to make certain that your daily mood and emotional state support good health."

Here are a few of the many physical benefits of laughter:

- *Laughter relaxes the whole body.* A good, hearty laugh relieves physical tension and stress, leaving your muscles relaxed for up to forty-five minutes after.
- *Laughter boosts the immune system.* Laughter decreases stress hormones and increases immune cells and infection-fighting antibodies, thus improving your resistance to disease.
- *Laughter triggers the release of endorphins.* Endorphins, the body's natural feel-good chemicals, promote an overall sense of well-being and can even temporarily relieve pain.
- *Laughter protects the heart.* Laughter improves the function of blood vessels and increases blood flow, which can help protect you against a heart attack and other cardiovascular problems.[39]

Wow Assignment

Investigate: For a week, observe and write down what makes your man smile, chuckle, laugh, and roll on the floor in stitches.

Invest: Buy some tools to keep humor in your love life: joke books, humorous videos, funny cards. Save the addresses of your favorite websites for jokes, video clips, or humorous blogs.

Implement: Every day do something that will make your man laugh. Or amp it up and email, text, call, or send him humor all day long the day of your big LOL date (see below).

Wow Wisdom

God really does have a sense of humor. Just look at the ostrich. Or how about the act of sex. Only someone with a funny bone could have come up with this system for procreating! Proverbs 17:22 emphasizes the upside of a smile: "A cheerful heart is good medicine."

Make a plan to tickle your man's funny bone. It'll make you both feel better.

Wow Date

Make a date to attend a musical comedy, visit a comedy club or Improv performance (www.improv.com), rent a funny video, or DVR a clean comedy special. Some resources for clean comedy are Outreach Comedians,[40] Cleancomic.com,[41] and Inspiring Comedy.[42]

Play It Again, Sam!

We were interviewed by a magazine on how to keep the fun and laughs in marriage. We didn't realize how much we have invested in this area until we were approached as "experts" in finding fun! Here are a few tips on making fun higher on your to-do list of ways to wow your man:

Be a Pal: What did you do with friends while growing up? Maybe you enjoyed things like bike rides, skateboarding, water or snow skiing, jet skiing, camping, rock climbing, hiking, board games, dancing, kite flying, Frisbee throwing, miniature golf. Anything you loved when you were young could bring some fun back into your love life today.

Be Prepared: Get some things on hand to serve as ticklers of your mate's funny bone: joke books, the Sunday comics, squirt guns, silly string, whoopee cushions—you're getting the picture. Put a few things in your desk drawer that could help lighten the load of your mate by providing comic relief.

I know this sounds like an oxymoron, but stock up so you can be spontaneous. If you are prepared, you can seize the moment! And a spontaneous attitude has its payoff. My friend Sharon spontaneously danced with her husband Mark in a Starbucks, and they were applauded by the British tourist enjoying their mocha magic.

Be Proactive: Schedule in fun as you would dentist or doctor appointments. If you have light at the end of your responsibility tunnel, the daily load is easier to bear. Another benefit of being the cruise director of your hubby's fun is that his heart will look forward to seeing you and spending time with you. Who would you rather see, the dentist or the cheerleader, an IRS agent or the masseuse? Easy call—you want the one who renews you, revives you, or releases your pain, not the one who inflicts it.

Be a Parrot: Make it your goal to remember those humorous things you see, things you say, jokes and stories you hear, signs, billboards, and bumper stickers you read. Some of our best laughs are when we run in from a lunch, a trip, or a meeting with a joke or story "you just have to hear." If you need to, write these down or use the recorder on your smartphone to help you remember the punch lines.

Wow Assignment

Set aside some time and some money to stock up for amusement. Make a list of activities your spouse enjoyed as a boy, as a teen, as a newlywed. You might need to interview his family and friends or casually ask your man about some of his happy memories. Pile up some books, magazines, toys, and novelties that might bring a smile to his face (garage sales can be a great source for guilt free enjoyment).

Wow Wisdom

Fill the storehouse! Joseph was elevated to second in command of Egypt because of the wisdom he shared to save for seven years so there would be a surplus in times of famine (Genesis 41). If you store up happy memories, when tough times come, your husband will find it easier to see the cup as half full and picture you as a friend not a foe.

Wow Date

Take your mate back to his boyhood. Invite your man out by attaching a note to a fishing pole, Ping-Pong paddle, or wrist rocket. Spend the afternoon skipping rocks while you tell stories or take a dip in a local pond after a picnic. Skate at a local park and take pleasure in sharing a banana split. Tousle his hair as you tickle his soul.

You might have to encourage your man to enjoy his loves. My friend Yvonne, when asked what was the most outrageously fun thing she had done with her honey, replied: "Zip lining in Alaska and parasailing in Hawaii. He didn't want to do either of them, but afterward he said it was the best of times...go figure."

Go play! Make it your goal to laugh until his sides split.

Be a Warrior, Woman!

Sometimes we just need to get our warrior woman on and fight for our man and fight for our marriage. I keep a broken board on a shelf in my office. It's from the day I earned my yellow belt in tae kwon do. It serves to remind me that "with God, all things are possible." I am, you are, stronger than we think we are.

In frontier days, women of the wagon trains might have to give birth on the trail. If they had a stillbirth, they would bury the newborn in the wheel tracks so as each wagon rolled over the grave, the dirt was packed down so the wild animals couldn't dig up the body. The woman would have to give birth, dig a grave, bury her child, then roll right on in order to get over the mountains before the freezing blizzards brought death. That is a tough woman. That is a woman who's willing to do whatever it takes for the good of her man and her family. She is a woman with a warrior spirit.

Being a courageous woman can be attractive. I led an all-women's kayak trip in the Alaskan wilderness with my friend Debbie, who is an award-winning outdoor educator. There is a fifty-fifty rule in Alaskan waters, which means if you are fifty feet from shore and you fall in, there's a fifty-fifty chance you won't survive. It takes some guts to get in the boat. For years after, Bill bragged to his friends about his courageous wife. To him, a woman in khakis and fleece is sexy.

Wow Assignment

How does your man need you to fight for him? How can you do battle for your future or your family? Are you willing to pinch pennies to save for his new business or education? Will you team up to combat with counseling an invasion of pornography that might have ensnared your man? Are you willing to enlist prayers to help move your man from the pit to the pinnacle? Are you willing to stick to your vows even if he is wavering on his? Will you face down the seductress of workaholism or the female coworker with her sights set on your man?

In my book, *Woman of Confidence*, I remind women of a quote by Mary Slessor: "God and one are a majority." Be brave. You and God are a winning military unit.

Wow Wisdom

We "good girls" have a hard time picturing ourselves as warrior princesses, but that is how God sees us. In Ruth 3:11, Boaz says to Ruth, "All the people of my town know that you are a woman of *noble* character." The word *noble* can be translated as a woman of "excellence"; a woman who has "strength of character"; a woman of "virtue"; "strong and mighty." It is used to describe King David's "mighty warriors" (1 Chronicles 11:10-11).

There's no need to use bullets, however. Prayer and persistence can win the battle.

Wow Date

To get in the right mindset, do something a little gritty, a little dangerous, a little edgy with your man. Attend a boxing or wrestling match. Go to a pistol range or karate class. Buy some camouflage and go hunting. Skydive or rock rappel.

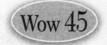

Ain't No River
High Enough

I am just a couple years shy of becoming a lifetime elite status frequent
flier member. It takes one million miles in the air to rack up this dis-
tinction. Many of those years I wasn't flying with my man, but no matter where my body might have been, I wanted my heart and mind to
remain where Bill was.

No amount of miles can pull your love apart if you maintain a little
creativity. Here are some ideas I have used to stay close in spite of being
miles apart:

- Sleep in his shirt.
- Take his picture for the hotel nightstand.
- Skype, text, call, or email consistently while gone.
- Jump right into his schedule and his life upon return, with
  or without jet lag.
- Stay emotionally plugged in to his world. I made it a point
  to know his schedule and priorities even if I was halfway
  around the world.

- Bring my experiences home for him to enjoy: spices to make the food of a foreign country, clothes of the locales, pictures or video that capture something I might be able to duplicate once I return.

Wow Assignment

Think like a travel agent. How can you stay emotionally close even if physically far away? Here are a few ideas from one of my female friends whose husband travels for missions nearly three hundred days a year:

- We send text messages that are either risqué or funny. Some are "hot," others key off of something funny that has happened.

- I slip notes and snacks into his suitcase.

- I sent the group he is with a photo and a paragraph about how much I love him, and they read it to him in front of the group. It said he was the best husband in the world… with apologies to the men there on the field.

Wow Wisdom

We spend a great deal of time encouraging the marriages of deployed military couples. The best advice for handling long stretches apart often comes from those who have successfully navigated it. Advice such as:

- Share the positives in your few minutes together on the phone or email. Don't talk about things he has no power or ability to do anything about.

- Read the same book together. If it contains discussion questions, use those to go deeper as you talk about issues the book raises.

- Once you are back together, set aside time to "make up for lost time." Handle reentry with fun first, and then work your way back into facing your responsibilities.

- Set a specific date to give back responsibilities of his that you handled while he was gone. Once you release them, leave them in his hands even if he does things differently than you would.

Wow Date

Another of my road warrior friends put a smile on her man's face when she shot a picture of herself holding a sign that covered her mid-section and read "Happy Birthday." The sign was strategically placed so it appeared as if she were in her birthday suit (even though she had on her bathing suit). Her husband texted back a smiley face.

Be innovative. Think of a date that brings where you have traveled home to him. When I traveled to Japan, I brought home matching kimonos, a paper Japanese lantern, and oriental music, and I invited Bill out on a Pacific Rim date by tucking a Japanese coin in his front pocket as I whispered, "Have I got a 'yen' for you!"

If you don't travel but wish you could, plan a date that will give a glimpse of the country you hope to one day take him to: pasta meal with opera playing; luau food by the pool; Chinese food and a Bruce Lee movie.

Wow 46

I Luv U

Texting can be one way to send the message, "Man, I want to wow you!" Send messages like:

- I heard someone whisper your name 2day, but wen i turned around 2 c who it was, i noticed i was alone, dats wen i realized it was my heart tellin me how much i miss U!

- Colors may fade, the sun may not shine, the moon may not be bright, heartbeats may stop, lives may pass but our friendship I'll treasure til the day my heart stops.

- There's a love that only u can give, a smyl dt only ur lips cn show, a twnkle dt cn only b seen in ur eyes, n a life of myn dt u alone can complete.

- Everyone wants 2 be the sun dat lights up your life. But I'd rather be ur moon, so I can shine on u during your darkest hour when your sun isn't around.

- Falling in love with you is the second best thing in the world. Finding you is the first.

- God is like a Hallmark card. He gave you to me as my FRIEND because He cares enough to send the very BEST.

- If I could be any letter in the alphabet, I'd choose V so I could be next to U. And if you could be any note, I wud wish you're RE so you're always beside MI![43]

Wow Assignment

Borrow a text, or better yet, create your own acronyms. The husband of one of my world-traveler friends was on an extensive trip to a country with sketchy Internet and phone coverage. She writes:

> Because I work at home, I'm often in my pj's. If my husband calls on Skype, that is sometimes interesting—especially if others are walking around behind him as he Skypes me! Once, he called and I was just out of the shower. But I didn't want to miss his call, so I rushed to my computer...yes, in my birthday suit. I didn't have time to even grab a towel. (I realized he had a roommate when the man walked behind my husband to the other side of the room...so I adjusted the camera up a bit for a more G-rated view.) We laughed and laughed, and he called me NCB (Naked Computer Babe) in text messages the entire three weeks he was gone!

Here are a few ideas for other acronyms:

- HH (Hot Hubby)
- Bill's might be GG (Grandpa Gorgeous)
- AMOG (Amazing Man of God)

What acronyms would be appropriate for your man?

Wow Wisdom

The Psalms are filled with short poems packed with meaning:

> O Lord, I love the habitation of Your house
> And the place where Your glory dwells.
>   (Psalm 26:8 NASB)

> I love God because he listened to me,
>   listened as I begged for mercy.
>
> (Psalm 116:1 msg)

It is possible to say a lot with few words.

Wow Date

Text through a date. Take a typical date but text love notes back and forth all night.

Text to a date. Use text messages to drop hints and clues to the next destination of a date that hops from place to place.

Put On Your
Construction Hat

There are times when, as a wife, you just need to put on all your protective gear and get in and rebuild. My friends Eric and Betsy had hit a tough spot in their relationship, and Betsy knew it was time to roll up her sleeves, dig deep, and get ready for plenty of overtime work to rescue her marriage. I appreciate Betsy because she was willing to fight for her love and her man. I think her husband best describes the holy spitfire in his honey:

> We were recently on a date night, going to see a traveling Broadway play. We went into a restaurant to kill an hour before the curtain time. The waitress, for whatever reason, was real demonstrative and kept touching my hand, my arm whenever she took our order or brought our corned beef and cabbage. I didn't really know what to do other than to keep my answers short and curt. When the waitress came back to drop off the bill and ran both hands up my back,

that was the final straw. Betsy called her over and whispered in her ear, accentuating her southern accent, "Sugar...you'd best leave my man alone!"

Wow Assignment

Betsy fought for her man and fought to rebuild her marriage after another woman set her sights on her husband. Eric continues:

Betsy confronted me and brought in the accountability of Bill [Farrel] as well as the marriage counselor we had been going to for three years. I was playing the game in counseling while living a duplicitous lifestyle. But when it was all discovered and came out, she played hardball. It forced me to make a decision and get off the fence. She also confronted the other woman because she had intercepted some inappropriate photos that the other woman took and emailed to me. I don't know how Betsy did it, but she got copies of these photo files as well as her husband's email and the email address of her adult children. She told the other woman "If you don't leave Eric alone, I'll send these photos to your husband, your adult children, and..." Once Betsy talked to her, she stopped immediately because she knew Betsy would follow through. Betsy fought for our marriage, and I think it made all the difference.

Does your man need you to roll up your sleeves and fight for his heart?

Wow Wisdom

The Bible calls us to admonish and to exhort, which are both aggressive, competitive words meant to bring about change. When you put the meaning of *admonish* and *exhort* together, you get a picture of a wife who walks alongside her husband, helping him see himself and life accurately and willing to love him in a way that brings out his best. When we stand up for our man, chances are he will want to be his best.

When I asked Eric what turned his heart back to his wife, he said:

> Her forgiveness. We were in such a season of turmoil. We argued all the time. I resented her success and became more and more angry and controlling. I also indulged in self-pity, which made me vulnerable to the enemy's attacks. The fact that Betsy would forgive me was more than I could comprehend. I knew it was the love of God through her, and that was worth giving up everything else to pursue.

Betsy's bravery accompanied with her words of assurance and forgiveness gave their love a second chance.

Wow Date

Betsy went the distance; she continued to fight for her love after the immediate crisis. She creatively dated her guy:

> I took Eric to the resort where we went when the spiritual intimacy returned after a dry season in our marriage. Years later, I secured the reservation and "kidnapped" Eric for a time of relaxation and rejuvenation. We also went to a classic theater from the 1940s to see a private screening of a movie he liked. There were 900 seats and only the two of us there![44]

What happy memory from the past can you use to build on for your future?

Wow 48

Be a Cheap Date

For many husbands romance seems frivolous, so if you can keep the costs down, your husband may enjoy your wow more. At www .Love-Wise.com, you'll find an article on "Recession Romance: 25 Free or Nearly Free Date Ideas," but here are a few more low-cost wow dates other women have suggested:

- "On our second date, I told my husband that he had 20 dollars and an evening out. How were we going to spend it? We scoured the newspapers and coupon books...ended up with dinner for two at El Pollo Loco, Dippin' Dots samples, miniature golf, bought some ice cream at the grocery store, went through a Jack in the Box for spoons, and sat on a hillside enjoying our ice cream."—Stephanie

- "We once went into a fancy clothing store and picked out a dream outfit for the other that we would never buy ourselves—just to try it on and see what the other would pick. It was fun and very telling about what he would love to see me wear."—Christina [Note from Pam: Bring a camera and take pictures.]

- "My sweet husband and I sell raffle tickets before show time at the local theater, and then we can stay and see the play for *free*."—Kristen

- "When the kids were little, and going out and getting a baby-sitter for four was out of the question, I would set a beautiful table for two in the living room by the fireplace—fancy dishes, the whole thing. Then I would feed the kids in the kitchen and get them up to bed. I would put on a fancy dress and greet my husband at the door. We would then have a candlelit dinner by the fireplace without the kids. It would give us a couple of hours alone. I still have the dress, and the kids refer to it as the 'date dress.'"—Nancy

- "Our favorite activity is to meet after work and walk a couple of miles in the shopping areas. It helps to de-stress and share what's on our minds. We stop for a bite and split a meal."—Connie

Wow Assignment

Make a jar, bottle, box, or bank that can collect pocket change to use for emergency dates. Make note of things that are entirely free but that speak love to your man. Perhaps if you wash his truck together and wear your bathing suit, that would wow him. There's zero cost.

Me? A bathing suit? I think not.

Okay, then maybe if you organize his tools, shine his shoes, or organize his junk drawer, that might wow him.

Wow Wisdom

We can learn from those who have experienced hard economic times yet kept a strong marriage. Who in your world has suffered a job setback, health issue, or other financial drain yet has a strong marriage? Look also to those from earlier generations who handled the depression or dust bowl years, the gas shortage of the seventies, or the high inflation of the eighties. Kelli looked to her own parents for inspiration:

I just pull from memory what my mother always told me that she and my dad used to do for fun during those times. My husband and I went to Sam's Club to pick up a few items, and instead of rushing in and out, we took our time. We held hands and went into the book section and looked at a few books...walked through the clothing pointing out what we liked. To hear him say, "Well, maybe I'll come back up here and get those socks for you for Christmas," was priceless. We looked at the furniture, testing out several rocking chairs, and I told him which chair I would buy him and he told me which table he would get me (one day, if or when we have the money), all the while sharing a drink as well as our likes/dislikes, thoughts, dreams, and hopes for the future. You could share a snack or an ice cream there. It may be a cheap date, but we had *more* fun that night than many a dinner/movie night. [Note from Pam: Plan it at dinner hour and dine just from the food sample booths spread out in these stores.]

Wow Date

This was the winning response to a contest I posted on my Facebook account for, "How to love on a shoestring budget":

> We each get $5 ($10 if we're lucky) and take turns going into a store—usually Walmart, KwikTrip, ACE Hardware, or Goodwill—while the other waits in the van. We each buy, without the other's knowledge, whatever we want for our "Date Night." Combining the two items into one date night is a hoot! He might buy a cup of worms and a six pack of Mountain Dew for a few hours of fishing—and I purchase a 1000-piece jigsaw puzzle.—Esthermay

Many of you collect pocket change on your dresser, in a jar, or a piggy bank. Break open the piggy bank, split the proceeds, and go on a date where you can each spend only the change you have in your possession.

On our favorite Valentine's date, we each had a five-dollar budget, and we divided up the letters of Valentine (Bill got *V*, I got *A*, and so on). I started my part of the date with A is for *Acting*, and we read a portion of *Romeo and Juliet* on a park stage. Think outside the Hollywood or Wall Street expectations of romance and create something truly unique with your pennies.

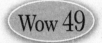
Wow 49

Honoring the Hard Times

Some of my favorite romantic movies are of women who love their man through something tough: the bank trying to take his farm, a man recovering from a devastating car crash and needing to learn to walk again, a woman who loves her guy through his battle with the bottle and back to sobriety.

My friend Carol loves like this. In one year, she lost her business and was diagnosed with breast cancer. Here is a snapshot of the way she loves even when things are tough:

> It had been decided. I would have a double mastectomy followed by a grueling course of sixteen chemotherapy treatments for breast cancer. My husband and I were understandably anxious. Neither of us knew what the next year would bring in terms of my health, our family life with our twelve-year-old son, our marriage, or our finances. He was unsure of the support I would require and whether he would be able to meet those needs. For a man who is really good at fixing things like screen doors and flat tires, the fact that

he couldn't fix this situation was frustrating and scary. Seeing his helplessness, I realized how much my cancer was also happening to him. Yet his pain was basically being ignored, while I was being showered with outpourings of love, kind words, and comforting prayer.

The night before my surgery we went out for a final nice dinner, not knowing when or if things would ever feel normal again. We ordered our meals and sat awkwardly for a few moments avoiding any show of overt emotion. Much to my husband's surprise, I handed him an envelope. "Why am *I* getting a card?" he asked. "Because your wife has cancer and that must be a very sad and scary thing for you," I answered as his eyes filled with tears. I wrote that I knew my cancer would be hard on him too and I was glad he would be at my side. I reassured him of my love and confidence in making it through together. While it was just a simple card, it made a huge difference to him. A big smile, albeit through tears, showed that his load had been lightened.

Wow Assignment

How has your man been affected by your sorrow or the pain of life? Think back through past years and note the trials and tribulations. Or survey the current landscape and see if you can detect any struggle or attack.

We live on a mountain. This past Christmas it rained for two weeks straight, and one morning we woke to a mudslide. Bill (and fortunately our grown sons) jumped up to spend the morning sandbagging to save our yard and a huge boulder from sliding down the hill and crushing homes (or people). They had to work hard to shore up the slope. How can you "shore up" your man?

Wow Wisdom

Carol's story is emotional and inspirational because she reflected Christ's example. Philippians 2:3-7 says:

Do nothing out of selfish ambition or vain conceit. Rather, in humility value others above yourselves, not looking to your own interests but each of you to the interests of the others. In your relationships with one another, have the same mindset as Christ Jesus:

> Who, being in very nature God,
>   did not consider equality with God
>   something to be used to his own advantage;
> rather, he made himself nothing
>   by taking the very nature of a servant,
>   being made in human likeness.

Humility is powerful in a marriage relationship. One of my favorite verses is Psalm 18:35, which in an earlier edition of the NIV says of the God who created us, "You stoop down to make me great." How can you humble yourself, bend down, stoop, or serve your man to help make him great?

Wow Date

Carol gives us one more idea on how to serve our man to make him great. Design an award:

> In addition to his full-time paying job, my husband has a nonprofit foundation where he gives tethered hot-air balloon rides to children and adults in wheelchairs. There are only four such equipped balloons in the country, and he is the only one that gives rides for free! While I am proud of his generous spirit and the joy that he brings, ballooning and the predawn hours it requires are not my thing. Because I don't embrace it as fully as he does, he (erroneously) felt I was not supportive of him. It was apparent my words of assurance weren't enough. Actions were going to be the only thing that would prove my support.
>
> Now I make a point to attend occasional balloon events

with him, even though I may sleep walk through parts of it. It is even better if I invite myself to accompany him before he can ask me. Recently, he hit a milestone of having given wheelchair balloon rides for ten years. To make sure he was duly honored, I put together a celebratory feast with fellow balloonists who fully appreciate the hard work he has put into the foundation. He got to revel in the retelling of past events and basked in the memories. That evening, in front of his peers, I awarded him with a medal that reads "Winner of a Million Smiles." Although he blushed, he wore it proudly, and when we returned home he conspicuously hung it on our fireplace mantel for all to see.[45]

Finish this sentence: I can reward my husband for being the world's greatest _____. Now come up with a way to celebrate your guy. Let this date be your version of his fantasy award ceremony.

Wow Words

Women often crave words of endearment and affirmation, but men value words too. Especially if those words help him feel sexy, invincible, strong, smart, or victorious. Lisa shares how something as simple as words can be empowering:

> The first year we bought our house we were living on a new budget, and I wanted something special for my husband's birthday. I bought a large piece of cardstock and wrote in small print with different colored markers all the reasons I loved him and made the shape into a heart. Some things were serious and others were, "I love you because you never once say, 'Why don't you clean out the litter box?' or 'Why isn't there any dinner tonight?'" He had a great time reading it and reliving all the memories and kept it out in the garage by his workbench until it eventually fell apart.

Lisa also created a place for words and symbols of her love:

> I bought a little red mailbox and I left it on our dresser. Each day during the month of February I left something in

it every morning. Some were cute poems or letters, other little gifts, photos, whatever. I tried to be creative, silly, and romantic. I think I had as much fun coming up with the idea as my husband did finding it.

Leah went above and beyond to get powerful words into her man's life:

My husband has friends all over the country, even a few in Europe. In a passing conversation, he mentioned how cool it would be to get all his friends together for a big birthday party, but how it would never happen and how sad it was that they would not all be together like that again.

I knew I could not make his wish come true, but with his birthday over two months away, I did the next best thing. I bought an oversized birthday card, and with the card, a ton of postage, some prepaid FedEx slips, and the list of people that I hacked from his computer, the "Great Birthday Chain Card Project" began. I had no idea if it would work, but I underestimated how awesome my husband's friends are and how much they cherish (not their word) his friendship.

The card made a few stops, and when it got to the town where he went to college, some alums that still live there not only signed it, but got his old football coach to sign it. When it got to his hometown, his family really got busy. Everyone from his first pastor to his Scout leader, Sunday school teacher, and even the first girl he ever kissed added their birthday greetings. It ended up, as planned, with his best friend, who overnighted it back to me with not a moment to spare.

I wish now that I had a video camera on him when he opened the card and slowly started to realize what had taken place. He still has the card, and both of us like to look at it now and then to see all the friends' good wishes and to remind him how special I and so many others think he is!

Wow Assignment

What words does your husband most need to hear from you now? Words that will:

- Build his hope for the future?
- Boost his self-confidence?
- Bolster his ability to succeed?

Make a list of words that capture the message he most needs to hear. You might begin with the phrase:

- Honey, I know things will get better because I remember amazing times with you in the past like...
- Babe, when I think of your best qualities, I think of...
- Sweetheart, with God's help you can...

Wow Wisdom

Holly shared the power words had in her husband's life:

> One year for our anniversary I bought a stack of heart-shaped sticky notes and wrote something on each one: "You can calm me like nobody else can," "I love your heart and your strength," "Thank you for being such a great father," "You make me feel special, thanks for your creativity and your attention." I stuck the hot-pink notes all over the shower door so he would see them right away. I can tell he liked them because he saved every one and even stuck a few of them on the inside of the medicine cabinet where they still stick today.

Commit to memory these wise words from the book of Proverbs:

> Gracious words are a honeycomb,
>> sweet to the soul and healing to the bones.
>>> (Proverbs 16:24)

Wow Date

Make this date all about words of affirmation. Move from place to place and give a new love letter or card at each location. Or create a wall of words, as in the movie *A Beautiful Mind*, and cover a wall, his car, the shower door, or your room with sticky notes of encouragement.

One Valentine's Day I put up a big pink poster at every location I thought Bill would go: shower door, back of the front door, on his windshield, on the front door of the church. Each one was a proclamation of what an amazing lover he is. They said things like "He is that great!" and "World's Best Lover."

Girls, get your pen out!

Voicemail

Our tone of voice, our words, can woo and wow our man—or rip him to shreds. Author Sharon Jaynes has a vivid example:

Catherine and I set out for a lazy summer stroll...Before I knew it, a few minutes turned into a couple of hours.

"Oh, my!" I exclaimed. "It's ten o'clock...I bet Steve's worried sick. He doesn't even know where I am. I'd better give him a call before I start back home."

When I dialed the number, the answering machine picked up. After I listened to my sweet Southern greeting, I left a bitter message.

"Steve, I was calling to let you know I'm at Catherine's. I thought you'd be worried, but apparently you don't even care because you won't even pick up the phone!" Click. I said my goodbyes to Catherine and left feeling somewhat dejected...

As my eyes adjusted to the darkness, I noticed someone coming toward me. It was Sir Galahad riding on his steed...his bicycle!

"Where have you been?" Steve desperately asked. "I've

been riding all over the neighborhood looking for you! Do you know what time it is?"

"Oh, you do care," I said with a grin, giving him a big hug...

When we got back home, I quickly erased the message on the machine before Steve could hear my reprimanding words. "Whew," I thought, "that was close."

A few days later, Steve called me from work.

"Sharon, have you listened to the answering machine lately?...I think there's something on there you need to hear."

The message on the answering machine went something like this.

(The voice of a Sweet Southern Belle) "Hello, you've reached the Jaynes' residence. We're unable to answer the phone right now...(Enter the voice of Cruella Deville) I was calling to let you know I'm at Catherine's. I thought you'd be worried, but apparently you don't even care because you won't pick up the phone! (Return of Sweet Southern Belle) At the sound of the beep, leave your number and we'll get back with you as soon as possible." Beep...

"Lord," I prayed. "This is so embarrassing."

"Yes, it is," He replied.

Wow Assignment

Like Sharon, I can often struggle with my "tone." Early in our marriage Bill risked to share with me how a certain tone I use wounds him to the core. Of course, I defensively replied, "What tone!" in the exact tone he was meaning. To really catch your own tone, carry around a tape recorder for just one day and listen to not just the words you use but the tone in which you use them.

Often people give clues that our tone is harsh:

- They step back.
- They close their eyes or tears well up in them.
- They leave the room—or the house.

There might be a reason your man spends so much time in the garage or with his buddies—your tone may be sending him there.

Wow Wisdom

Sharon continues:

> Well, [God] didn't really say that in so many words. It was more like this: "With the tongue we praise our Lord and Father, and with it we curse human beings, who have been made in God's likeness. Out of the same mouth come praise and cursing. My brothers and sisters, this should not be. Can both fresh water and salt water flow from the same spring?...Neither can a salt spring produce fresh water" (James 3:9-12).
>
> "OK Lord, I get the message," I prayed. But unfortunately, so did a lot of other people. [46]

Wow Date

What has your tone of voice been lately? Change your tone and let your man hear it. Call and leave a voicemail message inviting him out for some outrageous fun.

What words have you been using? Trade in any negative messages for some positive ones. Use a Scrabble board to spell out an apology or a love note. Buy a children's magnetic alphabet and spell out an "I love you" or an "I need you" message. Plan a date that features positive words, dinner at a jazz club, tickets to a romantic theater production, or best yet, say words he needs to hear, longs to hear, or thinks he might never hear:

- I was wrong.
- I am sorry.
- Please forgive me.
- Can we try again?

Double Date

When we were newlyweds, we knew one thing: "We have no idea what we're doing!" My wise husband stood in the back of the church one Sunday and looked around for a couple with a little gray hair that looked like they were still in love. He then sat us behind that couple. During the greeting time Bill asked, "You two look in love. How'd you do it?" They said the answer would take longer than the time the pastor gave for the greeting, and they invited us to lunch. It was great—free food and great advice! This began a pattern in our life of always spending time with mentor couples.

Bill and I know many amazing couples, so I thought I'd share some advice they have to offer:

> We don't say cruel or hurtful things to each other. We may get angry and need to vent...but we never stooped to wound each other by using demeaning names, belittling, or verbally abusing one another. True love includes empathizing with those you say you care about. We added commitment, forgiveness, and along the way, we discovered the sweetness and excitement a daily, ten-second kiss could

add to our marriage. The past forty years, even with all their challenges, have been so sweet that we'd marry each other again in a heartbeat!—Honorable Graydon W. Dimkoff and Jennie Afman Dimkoff

One year for our anniversary I decided to kidnap my husband. I rented a room at a nice hotel in town. In the afternoon I packed a suitcase for Mark, and I checked into the hotel. After I got the suitcase unpacked, I went home and prepared his anniversary card. I tucked the room key in the card. I told Mark I'd made dinner reservations at one of our favorite restaurants (which just happened to be at the hotel I'd already checked into). We enjoyed a great evening out, and I gave Mark his card when they brought dessert. Needless to say, we didn't go home that night.—Jill and Mark Savage, Hearts at Home Ministry

In her book, *My Heart's at Home*, Jill writes "The absolute best parenting strategy you and I can have is to make our marriage a priority. This gives our kids the security they long for…if Mom and Dad are okay, their world is okay."

After I gave birth to my daughter and my body returned to some level of normalcy, the last thing I wanted to do was to take off my clothes in front of my husband—lights on or off. I had gained 60 pounds during my pregnancy, and childbirth unloaded not much more than the 7.5-pound baby girl we adored. I would have been content with breastfeeding and mothering, postponing sex for the rest of my life or until I dropped 50 pounds, whichever came first.

Not my love-hungry husband, especially since the weight was coming off at a snail's speed. Fortunately, the Lord gave me a heart that loves a challenge and a mentor who reminded me that this time it was not about me—and that the most important sex organ I possessed was not my body but my mind. I decided right then and there that Victoria's Secret and I would give this neglected husband a "fishing night" to remember, which included our baby at grandma's house, a greeting sign at the door that read, "A fisherman lives here with the best catch of his life," candles leading the way to the "fishing dock," and the prize catch wrapped in fishnet stockings and lace.—Maria and Sam Keckler

Wow Assignment

What couple in your world has a love you can look up to? What skills do you need to learn? Who has overcome some of the obstacles that face your love? Now ask your husband these same questions. Make a list of four to five couples who might have something in their love you can learn from.

Wow Wisdom

The Bible encourages mentoring: "teach these truths to other trustworthy people who will be able to pass them on to others" (2 Timothy 2:2 NLT).

Wow Date

Make a double date with a couple who is stable, happy, seems to have a red-hot romantic life, and whose company you both enjoy. Do an activity the guys will enjoy, and then sit back and observe. You don't need to grill the couple, but feel free to ask them casual questions.

In mentoring relationships, often what is done, not what is said, makes the biggest impact. Watch what the wife says to and about her spouse; what she does for or with her man. See if you can pick up on any habits or choices your friend has made that might strengthen or improve your ability to wow your man and put a smile on his face.

Then wow him by walking out your new wisdom!

About the Author

Pam Farrel and her husband, Bill, are cofounders and codirectors of Love-Wise, an organization to help people connect love and wisdom and bring practical insights to their personal relationships. The Farrels are international speakers and authors of over 30 books including bestselling *Men Are Like Waffles—Women Are Like Spaghetti*, *Red-Hot Monogamy*, and *The 10 Best Decisions a Couple Can Make*. In addition, Pam has written numerous books for women including *The 10 Best Decisions a Woman Can Make*, *Becoming a Brave New Woman* (formerly *Woman of Confidence*), and *10 Secrets to Living Smart, Savvy, and Strong*. The Farrels are relationship columnists for several newspapers, magazines, and blogs and are frequent guests on radio and TV shows bringing relationship advice to people worldwide. They have been happily married over 31 years, are the parents to three children, and enjoy their relationship with their daughter-in-law and two young granddaughters. More about the Farrels and their resources can be found at *www.Love-Wise.com*.

Notes

1. Ginger Kolbaba, "Need Some Fun in Your Marriage?" *Today's Christian Woman,* September/October 2009, 29.

2. http://mattmclean.blogspot.com/2008/04/there-must-be-pony-in-here-somewhere.html.

3. Personal email from Catherine Hart Weber, PhD, author of *Flourish: Discover the Daily Joy of Abundant, Vibrant Living* and *Secrets of Eve: Understanding the Mystery of Female Sexuality.*

4. Danielle Turner, "Surprise, Surprise!" The Naked Scientists: Science Radio and Naked Science Podcasts (www.thenakedscientists.com/HTML/articles/article/daniturnercolumn2.htm/).

5. Carole Lewis, *A Thankful Heart* (Ventura, CA: Regal Books, 2005).

6. For a fuller discussion of this, see our book *The Marriage Code* (Eugene, OR: Harvest House Publishers, 2009).

7. "How Are Diamonds Cut if They Are the Hardest Substance?" (www.wisegeek.com/how-are-diamonds-cut-if-they-are-the-hardest-substance.htm). Medieval diamond cutters cut their cleaved stones with other diamonds, lubricating the surfaces with oil and grinding away at the stone to reveal facets. Some diamond cutters still use other diamonds as part of their cutting and polishing process.

8. You can find more on money motivation and budgets on the articles page of our website: www.Love-Wise.com. Look under the heading Free Resources.

9. Catherine Rampell, "Money Fights Predict Divorce Rates," *New York Times,* November 24, 2010 (http://economix.blogs.nytimes.com/2009/12/07/money-fights-predict-divorce-rates/).

10. Gail E. Hudson, "Money Fights," www.coeinc.org/AllPages/Materials/Articles/Articles/PDF%20Files/MoneyFights.pdf.

11. www.efmoody.com/longterm/lifespan.html.

12. Median age of widowhood according to 1996 U.S. Census: www.census.gov/prod/2002pubs/p70-80.pdf.

13. http://marriagejokes.net/secret_to_getting_the_last_word.html.

14. Personal email from K!mberly Creasman to Pam, December 1, 2009. To learn more about the Creasmans' ministry visit www.crmleaders.org.

15. Robert A. Emmons, "Practicing Gratitude Can Increase Happiness by 25%," *Psychblog,* September 10, 2007 (www.spring.org.uk/2007/09/practicing-gratitude-can-increase.php).

16. Personal email from K!mberly Creasman to Pam.

17. The psalmist in 119 works his way through the Hebrew alphabet to recount the goodness and greatness of God and God's Word.

18. http://blog.gaiam.com/quotes/topics/idiosyncrasies.

19. www.scribd.com/doc/41931/You-Know-Youre-Addicted-To-Coffee-If-.

20. Positively Coffee: www.positivelycoffee.org/%2ftopic_driving_statement.aspx.

21. Postively Coffee: www.positivelycoffee.org/topic_exercise_statement.aspx.

22. http://men.webmd.com/features/coffee-new-health-food.

23. http://men.webmd.com/features/coffee-new-health-food.

24. http://answers.yahoo.com/question/index?qid=20070402223745AABTSZA.

25. Adapted from http://science.nationalgeographic.com/science/space/solar-system/full-moon-article.html.

26. Laurie Puhn, "Love and Sex: The Secrets of Close Couples," *Women's Health*, Jan/Feb 2011, 106.

27. http://en.wikipedia.org/wiki/Puzzle.

28. Ibid.

29. www.baselinemag.com/c/a/Business-Intelligence/25-Fast-Facts-About-Twitter-in-the-Workplace-212013/.

30. Account name is PamFarrel (no space).

31. Lev Grossman, "Person of the Year 2010, Mark Zuckerberg," *Time,* December 27, 2010, 50.

32. Ibid., 72.

33. www.emaxhealth.com/1357/women-checking-facebook-going-bathroom.

34. Grossman, "Mark Zuckerberg," 72.

35. http://mashable.com/2010/08/28/facebook-narcissism/.

36. Ibid., 61, 67.

37. Email from Jody Saranpa to Pam, August 2010.

38. Personal email from Julie Schaecher.

39. Laughter is the Best Medicine: http://www.helpguide.org/life/humor_laughter_health.htm.

40. www.outreach.com/events/christian-comedians.aspx.

41. www.christiancomic.com.

42. www.inspiringcomedy.com/christian-comedians/.

43. http://romantictexts.blogspot.com/.

44. Private email used by permission. Names have been changed to protect privacy.

45. Carol Murphy. I'm happy to report that Carol survived the cancer. Thank God, we need women like her to remind us how to love.

46. Sharon Jaynes, "Mixed Messages," Girlfriends in God, October 1, 2010 (www.girlfriendsingod.com/Devotions/DevotionArchives/2010DevotionArchives/October10Devotions/MixedMessages10110/tabid/955/Default.aspx).

Other Harvest House Books by the Farrels

THE 10 BEST DECISIONS A WOMAN CAN MAKE
Finding Your Place in God's Plan

Women today have important decisions to make about family, career, and ministry. Sometimes the daily choices seem overwhelming. Popular author and speaker Pam Farrel encourages women to discover the joy of finding their place in God's plan as they

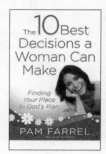

- stop pleasing people and start pleasing God
- find a positive place to direct their creativity, energy, and enthusiasm
- gain confidence about the value of their time and efforts
- assess their strengths and weaknesses, skills, and talents

Pam's motivating, liberating message will empower women to pursue God's best for their life.

This popular book, now with a fresh new cover for today's readers, includes a study guide and discussion questions for personal or small group use.

10 SECRETS TO LIVING SMART, SAVVY, AND STRONG
Rerelease of *Fantastic After 40!*

Pam Farrel points the way for women in midlife to live smart, savvy, and strong during this exciting and demanding season. Insights on relationships, health, menopause, finances and more are infused with biblical wisdom and loads of humor. Readers will discover how to

- trust in God in more fulfilling ways with life-impacting decisions
- be at peace with new physical, mental, and emotional changes
- benefit from diet, exercise, and relationships to maximize midlife and beyond

Designed for personal or group study, *10 Secrets to Living Smart, Savvy, and*

Strong will empower those baby-boomer women who seek life-enhancing wisdom and want to pass it along to others.

> "Pam Farrel brings her energy and enthusiasm to the subject of aging joyfully with wisdom that is both sassy *and* sage. Pam's life experience and biblical insight give us an internal GPS with a friend's voice. Seasoned Sisters, unite! Fan yourselves! And treat yourself to this delightful book from a girlfriend's girlfriend!"
>
> — Anita Renfroe, comedian and author of
> *If It's Not One Thing, It's Your Mother*

Men Are Like Waffles—Women Are Like Spaghetti
Understanding and Delighting in Your Differences

With 150,000 copies sold, bestselling authors Bill and Pam Farrel deliver biblical wisdom, solid insight, and humorous anecdotes—all served up in just the right combination so that readers can feast on enticing ways to

- keep communication cooking
- let gender differences work for—not against—them
- help each other relieve stress
- achieve fulfillment in romantic relationships
- coordinate parenting so kids get the best of both Mom and Dad

The Farrels explain why a man is like a waffle (each element of his life is in a separate box) and a woman is like spaghetti (everything in her life touches everything else). End-of-chapter questions and exercises make this unique and fun look at the different ways men and women regard life a terrific tool for not only marriage, but also for a reader's relationships at work, at home, at church, and with friends.